*Pumla Gqola's mind exhilarates. The to
book is as conversational as it is probing
insight open up page after page with da
literary presence that makes thinking a pleasure.*

Njabulo S Ndebele

*Is Simphiwe Dana full of contradictions? Without a doubt. But
so are the rest of us. What sets her apart is that she is not only a
genius, according to the author, but a renegade. The book is an
exploration of this theme in the public life of Dana: the musician
vs. the social activist; the feminist vs. the tabloid sleaze fodder...
The author looks for the meaning of Dana's music and distils the
answer to: "our insides matter". This portrait of Dana – it is not a
biography – derives its charm, and occasional irritation, in that the
author is a self-confessed fan and friend of the artist. It is a timely
square in the quilt that is Simphiwe Dana, an outstanding artist of
her generation.*

Lizeka Mda

*Near every sentence in this book is a piece of soul music. I was
left impressed, envious, and excited. While it claims to be about
thinking of Simphiwe Dana out loud, the book is really a beat
for millions of gifted, young, uncontainable Simphiwes who dare
reimagine our society. I know of very few scholars who can make
feminism sound so clear, enjoyable, hip, right and black, all at
once.*

Kopano Ratele

In A Renegade Called Simphiwe, *Dana is described as being a planet, rather than a star. If so, then this book is the tidal flow that both reveals and conceals that planet. It wonderfully mimics the contradictions that its subject embodies, blending the passionate play of emotional involvement with the rigour of academia to produce a book that is both a pleasure to read and a spur to introspection.*

Chris Roper

A Renegade Called Simphiwe

A Renegade Called Simphiwe

Pumla Dineo Gqola

First published by MFBooks Joburg, an imprint
of Jacana Media (Pty) Ltd, in 2013

10 Orange Street
Sunnyside
Auckland Park 2092
South Africa
+2711 628 3200
www.jacana.co.za

ISBN 978-1-920601-08-9

Cover design by publicide
Author photograph by Victor Dlamini
Set in Sabon 11/15pt
Printed and bound by Ultra Litho (Pty) Ltd, Johannesburg
Job No. 001989

See a complete list of Jacana titles at www.jacana.co.za

For my parents, Thato and Dambile, with all my love,
and in deepest gratitude

Contents

For my own engagement with images, I often prefer less information, some blurryness, some grey areas, some wonderment/ questions... I am attempting to open up a variety of possibilities to the readings, or even destabilise some clear-cut fixed positions. I think people are often annoyed by the blurriness, so whether this strategy works is anyone's guess.

Ingrid Masondo

Think it through. Being human means there are decisions you may not survive.

Simphiwe Dana

Our visions begin with our desires.

Audre Lorde

Acknowledgements

Although one person sits in front of her computer to write the many words that eventually become a book, a book is also the result of many others' efforts. I am extraordinarily blessed to have many people in my life who made writing this book possible through various forms of support, listening, loving and pushing.

Melinda Ferguson, thank you for asking me to write my dream project as part of the first five books on your imprint. Thank you for your faith in me and the freedom that only a writer can bestow on another. As importantly, thank you also for the courageous inspiration in your life choices to face some odd and scary places within myself. I know I have tested your patience and almost lost both our minds in the process, but I appreciate you more than you know.

Simphiwe Dana, thank you for the magical music, for your beauty and for your generous spirit, all of which inspired this book. I hope some of what lies between these pages feels true to you.

I am eternally grateful for my writer friends who put up with my endless talking about the book, instead of writing it. Gail Smith, as usual, let me go on many tangents, affirmed me and loved me. Thank you for doing such a wonderful job of co-mothering our son. Dina Ligaga, for always pretending I am much more interesting than I am, for teaching me so much and for being gentle with me. Sarah Chiumbu, for always telling me what you think, being generous with your heart and time. Angelo Fick, Yethu's uncle, who will not agree with me on any popular culture topic but has given me almost two decades of love, laughter and the best intellectual conversations.

Thozama Vokwana, Thumeka Scwebu Sibulela, Unathi Conjwa Mdlungu, thank you for being constants in my life. Thozie, I can't wait to hold your book in my hands soon. Putuma Patrice Gqamana, our conversations and your friendship truly feed my spirit.

My wonderful brother, Sizwe, who brought his friend and my chosen brother Mandla to the last book launch and lets me complain about writing *ad nauseam*. I do hope you make more time for your own writing in the midst of your exciting life. My brilliant sister, Viva, who never gets tired of reading endless bits and pieces from me or of playing the same games with me. Amazing Lebo, who has always believed I could achieve things more spectacular than my wildest dreams. Big sisters don't come better than you. Ncumisa, my chosen sister and oldest friend, who bought multiple copies of my previous book and pretended to buy them for a range of people I have never heard of. Tat' uTshezi, my daddy's best friend, thank you, Tenza, for calling me to tell me how proud you are of me when it matters, since Daddy's passing on.

Khalo Matabane who laughed at me when I was having mini-crises about nothing and convinced me to laugh too. George Lwanda who shared his tastes in non-fiction titles with me, made me laugh until I cried, and reminded me that generosity should only be met in kind. Thank you for both embodying your middle name and also for holding up a mirror to my face when that was the last thing I wanted to look into. Thank you for helping me make the decision to join the rooms that are saving my life one day at a time.

Shireen Hassim who always knows exactly what to say even when I haven't seen her in months and we are both rushing in opposite directions. Nomntu Mali, thirty-one years after first meeting you, I still want to be you when I grow up. Prudence

Mabena, Thandisa Nkonyeni and Puleng Shirley Koaho, friends of my youth who have come back into my life with such grace, insight and magic as I wrote this book and continue to teach me, makes me a better person and therefore writer.

Achieng and Zuri Ojwang who came to pick Yethu up for an outing that turned into a sleep-over, and Nonceba Ludidi for lovingly taking our sons on so many elaborate excursions as I wrote. Achieng and Nonceba, I am delighted by your friendship. Sithabile Ndlovu, my life would be utter chaos without you. Thank you for being the other mother to my son for these past five years.

Thank you, Grace A. Musila, who edited this manuscript with the grace of a writer and her signature generosity intellectually and personally.

And finally, to my angel boy, Yethu, who fills my heart with utter bliss every single day. I promise we can google image superheroes many times a day again now that Mama is not 'always working on the book'. And I am really sorry we lost Menisana.

Preface

In the last decade, I have been fascinated by the ways in which South Africa seems to be experiencing what I have now taken to calling 'a creative explosion'. I have been amazed by how many really daring artists exist at this time who so brazenly create a new mould, mess with older patterns and are at the same time truly outstanding in their craft. This explosion is hard to pin down because it is not so much a school, nor can we really chalk it up to the arrival of a democracy that has freed up the imagination. Let's face it, South African reality is very often much stranger than fiction, as many writers in the seventies and eighties often commented. Some cynics argue that novels and theatre ticket sales are so low because the newspapers and news bulletins have so many bizarre stories that ordinary people's appetites are satiated. I am not convinced.

There are some really exciting ways of thinking about ourselves as individuals and as a society that are being suggested in the works of several artists working today. In certain disciplines in the academy, we study various arts and take both the structure and content of certain arts seriously. But we seldom talk to each other across the boundaries of these creative arts: music, literature, theatre, film, fine art, photography, digital arts, and so forth. Those of us who move between different artistic spaces also notice their insularity all the time. I am not just speaking of the academy.

It often strikes me at an exhibition that the artists are grappling with issues that some writers in the same city are also exploring, but often the two groups have never met and have no familiarity with each other's work. It would be so electrifying to speak across these boundaries sometimes. This inspiring conversation across boundaries does occasionally happen. Sociologist Shireen Ally's book launch was an excellent exploration of this. At the 2010 Johannesburg launch of *From Servants to Workers: South African domestic workers and the democratic state,* she invited novelist Zukiswa Wanner and visual artist Mary Sibande as her co-panellists. Ms Wanner's debut novel *The Madams* and Ms Sibande's Sophie from *Long Live the Dead Queen* series revisit the ever-present, hyper-visible domestic worker figure and presence in urban South Africa. More recently, in her performance on the place of love in world altering politics staged at the Windybrow Theatre in November 2012, Mmatshilo Motsei brought a painter and a dancer on stage with her. There is also the notable collaboration between poet Kgafela oa Magogodi and filmmaker Jyoti Mistry on *I Mike what I Like* (2006). It does not happen often enough. At the same time, such collaborations are not easy for artists or audiences due to our limited, medium-specific literacies. I battled with aspects of poet Lebogang Mashile's 2008 collaboration with Moving into Dance Mophatong as much as I did with Motsei's show because I struggle to make sense of professional dance. Yet, difficulty is an opportunity to try out different ways of making sense.

What might it mean to have a conversation about an artist in the same ways that we have conversations about politicians, activists or celebrity gangsters, in the same public domain that their art circulates? This book is my engagement with this question, as a writer in conversation with the ideas in another artist's work.

Simphiwe Dana is the artist I wanted to have this conversation on paper with the most. When Melinda Ferguson and I first met to discuss writing this book, she cautiously offered me the opportunity to write my dream book. She offered it cautiously, I imagine, as both a writer and a publisher. Writers do not really like being told what to do; writer-Melinda was sensitive to this. In her new publisher's hat, she could not switch off her internal writer voice even though she had a vision for the range of titles she wanted for an imprint that bore her name. I was flattered that she wanted me to write one of the first few books in her exciting new imprint, MFBooks Joburg. That excitement has not died down as I write this.

When she first burst onto the scene in 2004, with her debut album *Zandisile*, Simphiwe Dana offered various aesthetic challenges to her audiences. That album appealed to listeners who may not ordinarily dance together. Simphiwe's music charmed jazz audiences who recognised a familiar jazz aesthetic in her sound. Yet the wit and playfulness in her debut album also delighted kwaito fans and admirers of what was increasingly being labelled Afropop. Her artistry grasped at the serious without compromising on pleasure. She mesmerised South Africans through the airwaves that year, alongside various other artists who were musically hard to pin down, like Thandiswa Mazwai's debut solo offering *Zabalaza* and MXO, whose 2004 album *Piece of Mind* was classified Afropop although its acoustic, rock-meets-hip-hop stretched that label. It was 2004, the year that marked a decade of South Africa's democracy, and although the country was not utopia, the hope for what the country could still become was palpable. Kwaito and, more recently, the Afropop of groups like Mafikizolo and Malaika had been the sound of the times. While the star power of these groups would remain deep-rooted well into the second decade of democracy, there was also a hunger for something more. Although Simphiwe Dana makes sense when located in the musical traditions populated by Miriam Makeba, Busi Mhlongo, Ringo Madlingozi, her peers MXO and other Afropop/Afrosoul artists, her voice and politics are also very distinct.

The book is called *A Renegade Called Simphiwe* because Simphiwe widens many people's senses of what is appropriate and imaginable. She is a rebel even within defiant spaces. Simphiwe Dana is simply not interested in adhering to conventional ideas about where to live, who to love or how to write. One minute

South Africa worships at her throne. The next minute, we are trying to rein her in. This says something about her, as someone whose investment in trying out what interests her, and living her truth trumps risking societal censure. It also says something about South Africa's sensibilities. As a renegade, Simphiwe does not play safe.

This book is a writer's portrait in words, a writer thinking out loud. I have had moments of utter joy writing it. And there have been times when I just did not want to write it anymore. In between were weeks where I could not write a word and would not let myself. Life has also happened in the space between writing as well as through those spaces. I have written the bulk of this book whilst going through a major life transformation and it has tested precisely that which I seek to transform. Midway through writing this book, I was finally rewarded with the strength to confront a personal demon of many years that I had been working hard to get the emotional strength to face. The rewards of that second process have given me peace of mind for the first time since I was a child. Perhaps the decision to write a book that I simply wanted to write, which does not really translate clearly into any of the writing personalities or ambits I am comfortable occupying, had something to do with this.

Finally, I try to write what I would like to read. This is hardly original, but I have found that, as a reader, I often find value in books other writers felt compelled to write.

CHAPTER 1

No paradox:
A renegade's community

How can you not believe in your own brilliance,
Black girl, at a time when the face of genius is
Lebogang Mashile, Thandiswa Mazwai, Zanele
Muholi, Gabeba Baderoon, Zukiswa Wanner,
Xoliswa Sithole and Simphiwe Dana?

For a few years, I would ask this rhetorical question from my literature and media students at the university where I profess as part of teaching critical thinking about power through creative forms. It is a question that many of the students have commented on subsequent to this. When I asked this question, I was not saying this is the exclusive face of brilliance. I was drawing attention to the importance of thinking against the grain, encouraging an intellectual and political stance that functions differently from the dominant messages that Black girls and women are given about themselves, about ourselves, in contemporary South Africa and beyond. I was pointing out that, as brutal as South Africa, and South African public discourse, often is to young Black women, there was a certain type of woman artist who was achieving the previously unimaginable. As real as the policing of women's bodies is in South Africa, and the world, it is possible for women to think of themselves – of ourselves – differently. It is important that a critique of power not end with reaction, but that it goes further to imagine something new, more exciting, more pleasurable. Picture what we can *create* if we dare give ourselves permission to imagine freely.

It is important to create alternatives just like it is necessary to speak truth to power. These need not even be separate processes, as the women artists above demonstrate.

This question, then, was one of a series of invitations to my students to look for what else is happening in the world around them, to choose to think differently about themselves. The artists whose names I listed – and sometimes the names were different from the ones noted here – embody something important to flag to these young people.

I am not just talking about having someone wonderful who looks like you available for emulation, what we sometimes call a role model, although there is nothing wrong with role models. They are to the spirit what air is to the body, to ordinary people what a muse is to artists: a generative life force. Role models, as people whose lives encourage you to live the one you want, to pursue the dreams you may not yet be able to say out loud, are crucial. Although it has become somewhat fashionable to use the tag 'role model' contemptuously, I continue to believe that their presence cannot be overstated. A role model is someone who affirms your desire to be more of yourself by mere virtue of living your own life courageously and joyfully. It makes sense to me that the women I listed should be role models, whether they actively set out to exist in this capacity or not. In any event, you do not choose to be a role model so much as people bestow the compliment on you as you go about your business.

When I listed the names above, I did not mean to highlight only the overlapping prominence, fame and genius. Yes, it matters that my students will recognise these names. It matters at least as much, although sometimes *more,* that each of these women is a game-changer. Game-changers are a breed of innovators who not only create something new, but shift the reference point on a certain matter or in a field. In other words, game-changers do more than come up with an exciting new product or way of doing things. Such discovery also changes the context of the innovation. These women are all courageous artists who dared produce and release publicly the kinds of visionary material that we did not have before. They are not just emulated and imitated on a daily basis; they have changed the rules of the game. And in the midst of contradictory messages about who they are, their value and their place in South African society, they survive. I see Simphiwe Dana as this kind of artist, and this kind of woman. Women artists like her are not the same person, carbon copies of each other, but they are products of this time and offer immense possibilities to think transformatively about ourselves and this time, on this part of earth that we live in.

Poet Lebogang Mashile often notes that as difficult as it is to think against the grain, and to pursue what you desire as a creative-intellectual in South Africa today, this time and place also offers possibilities that she cannot see elsewhere. In other words, there is something about South Africa *right now* that is making these artists possible, even if the response to their existence is not always as receptive and sophisticated as it could be.

I now turn to elaborate briefly on each of these women as part of my larger argument about Simphiwe's place in our society.

Lebogang Mashile is the face of South African poetry. She is as magical in spoken word performance as she is elegant on the written page. As part of Feela Sistah, the poetry group that also comprised Ntsiki Mazwai, Napo Masheane and Myesha Jenkins, Mashile was key to shifting the largely male landscape of South African poetry to the current stage where the most prolific, exciting, productive poets are predominantly women. She is part of that generation that is unwavering in using its gift, profound intellect and sense of integrity to speak the unfashionable that nonetheless needs to be heard. Her presence in the public realm, painful though responses to her sometimes are, has been transformative and inspirational. Her

3

television magazine programme, *L'atitude* presented an exciting fusion of beauty, critical commentary, creativity and diversity, initiating a formula that we would see repeated over the years with no accreditation in television programmes from *Precious Africa* to *A country imagined*. The popularity of the initially largely unknown Mashile testified to a phenomenon we have yet to grasp, intellectually, mired as we are in lazy diagnoses of 'apolitical youth' and 'dumbing down' of popular culture. This much patronised generation made *L'atitude* one of the most watched programmes even though this magazine programme was decidedly unglamorous in its topics, which encompassed menstruation, genocide, language death, the Jacob Zuma rape trial and cycles of complicity by the left, religious intolerance, spirituality and virginity testing. Furthermore, Mashile, as producer and presenter of the show, presented an inspirational image of femininity as narrator: a healthy-bodied, natural-hair-rocking, fresh-faced, opinionated femininity. Often without make-up, this young woman who asked difficult questions while showing a range of unscripted emotions on national television, then wrote and read a poem to wrap up each show. Mashile's striking good looks and warm personality radiated off the television screen, but audiences were enchanted by more than her looks in an industry that is known for the high premium it places on beauty. Here, she achieved the difficult to explain: making feminist television the prime time viewers' choice.

Her versatility has also led to her being cast in her debut acting role in the Academy Award-nominated film, *Hotel Rwanda*, a role in the 2008 Standard Bank National Arts Festival performance of an adaptation of K Sello Duiker's 2001 novel *The Quiet Violence of Dreams*, and her multi-faceted collaborative pieces with choreographer Susan Glaser to produce *Threads* in celebration of Moving into Dance Mophatong's 30th anniversary celebration, which also went to the 2009 Grahamstown Arts Festival. She has admitted to not really knowing what the Noma Award was until after she received a phone call informing her that she would be the 2006 recipient of the premier award for African writing. Her critical acclaim transcends well beyond South Africa's borders.

Thandiswa Mazwai is the supremely talented musician who debuted as the woman vocalist for the kwaito group, Bongo Maffin in 1998. Bongo Maffin, my favourite music group of all time, released six award-winning albums before unofficially splitting up in the mid noughties. There was no announcement of a formal split, and their website still describes them as a group, but they have not toured or released an album together in over a decade. Although many struggled to categorise the group's music, in interview after interview, kwaito was the deliberate label Bongo Maffin members chose, much to the chagrin of those pockets of their fans who thought kwaito was something to be disowned in favour of something deemed more refined like Afrosoul or jazz. In one television interview with a weekend show, a very young Mazwai declared kwaito to be a lifestyle in the same idiom that hip-hop was, while the three young men who formed part of her group, Stoan, Appleseed (later Jah Seed), and Speedy, nodded in agreement. This claim to kwaito was deliberate identification given with as much confidence as the advanced musical choices reflected in the group's music.

Following the break-up of the hugely successful group, Thandiswa Mazwai has enjoyed the most successful solo career out of the three, since Speedy had left Bongo Maffin a few years prior to Mazwai's solo release. Her debut solo album, *Zabalaza* (2004), reached double platinum and raked in numerous awards, which included two Kora Awards, three South African Music Awards (SAMAs) and a Metro FM Award. Her second album and DVD, *Ibokwe* (2009) went gold within six weeks.

Mazwai's natural great looks, with her increasing array of intricate hairstyles, which are artworks in and of themselves, and her dimples, offer her a canvas on which to play with notions of beauty in performance. Her body on stage is a canvas on and through which she plays with notions of identity, femininities, movement, Africanness and possibility. Being in the presence of Ms Mazwai performing live is to experience an explosion of the senses.

Her musical genius and adventurous spirit are staged equally through the collaborations she chooses, as in her subject matter. Although nuanced, her politics are unambiguous to the attentive listener. Such politics are clear in her musical repertoire across time, in her sound and lyrics. They reverberate in her careful choices about which musicians she opts to work with. In interviews, she speaks about the importance of releasing work that is both musically full of integrity and that represents her real vision for each project. She is involved in all aspects of her music and, as I write this, is in the middle of a country-wide search for an all-woman band. This is part of her renowned generosity and commitment to nurturing new talent.

I remember her response to comments on her careful Facebook status update expressing both admiration and concern for the young South African musician Zahara, when the artist first gained prominence in 2012. Mazwai had expressed her wish that the newer musician be allowed the space to be the kind of artist and person she wanted to be even with the glare of the media and new fans. In a global patriarchal culture obsessed with reading women's relationships as primarily adversarial, some responded with corrective sentiments about how Mazwai should not feel threatened by new artists since she was established. Thandiswa Mazwai's next update pointed out that there was room for many different kinds of women artists in the world, and that as a feminist, she had taught herself to relate to other women in non-competitive ways. Therefore, she was asserting that her concern was genuine and suggesting that there was room to read it as such.

There are endless questions and much speculation about Mazwai's private life, but she has control over what is said about her. Her Twitter presence is another manifestation of this carefully crafted presence: fiercely intelligent, humane and witty. Managing a very active performance schedule domestically and abroad, she speaks her mind on a range of topics. As present in the public eye as she has been from so young, how does she manage to avoid scandal so well? Whatever the answers are to this question, it is in no small measure to the level of control she exercises over her own life and the boundaries of what is public and private.

Zanele Muholi is a multiple award-winning artist who has recently and somewhat reluctantly accepted this title. For a long time, Muholi stressed her activist identity and insisted that her camera was simply one of a range of tools she uses in the pursuit of a more just society. Co-founder, with Donna Smith, of Forum for Empowerment of Women (FEW), the Black feminist lesbian NGO in Johannesburg, Muholi's work challenges ways of seeing Black lesbians and, increasingly, other queer people. Initially concerned with rendering Black lesbian lives visible by casting a spotlight on the many layers of violence such women face for their sexual orientation, Muholi has constantly sought to complicate the ways in which women's bodies, sexual orientation, violence and pleasure are imagined.

Muholi has had numerous group and solo exhibitions nationally, continentally and across the globe in the last decade. Her work has also garnered her awards such as the Casa Africa Award for best female photographer and the Jean-Paul Blanchere Award, both at the Bamako Biennale for African Photography (2009); the Fanny Ann Eddy prize for her outstanding contribution to the study of sexuality in Africa (2009); a Tollman Award for the Visual Arts (2005) and she has participated in the Venice Biennale (2011).

Her work is both an attempt to create an archive of images of varied Black women's bodies, sexual expressions and identities and the crafting of new ways of seeing. While the former is something she deliberately foregrounded in her early work – visually chronicling Black women's ways of loving – it is only recently that she has admitted to the presence of the latter in her photographs and short films. Muholi's vision is at once startling, humane, questioning, archival and generative.

Responses to her work have been complex. Her exhibition openings across the country see much larger numbers of out Black lesbians, gay, bisexual, transgender and intersex folk in attendance from outside the art world than most. When in 2010 the then South African Minister of Arts and Culture Lulu Xingwana made the *faux pas* of dismissing Muholi's and Nandipha Mntambo's work as not speaking to Black women's real lived experience, the outrage

7

from the Black (and wider) Lesbian, Gay, Bisexual, Transgender, Intersex (LGBTI) community was obvious in the public responses that emanated from this sector and community. Press releases from various NGOs such as FEW, Gender DynamiX, the Joint Working Group's open letter to Minister Xingwana, as well as opinions published in the newspapers by Gabeba Baderoon, Gail Smith, Phylicia Oppelt, Eusebius McKaiser and myself, among many others, asserted the importance of Muholi's vision. She is clearly deeply connected to the community she comes from, and continues to be active in many capacities although she no longer co-leads FEW.

Gabeba Baderoon is a celebrated poet and scholar. Her debut collection of poetry *The Dream in the Next Body* (2005) sold out in and went into reprint within six weeks, and had gone into its third reprint a year later, making not only South African literary history but also marking historic achievement and unprecedented success, especially for a writer who had only recently forayed into poetry. This same book saw her awarded the Daimler Chrysler Award for South African Poetry in 2005. It was also named a 'notable book of 2005' by the *Sunday Independent* and was a *Sunday Times* 'recommended book' the same year. Her next two collections were *The Museum of Ordinary Life* (2005) and *A Hundred Silences* (2007), and she also has a collection *The Silence before Speaking*, which brings together poems from the first two collections, and elsewhere, all translated into Swedish. *A Hundred Silences* was short listed for both the 2007 University of Johannesburg Prize and the Olive Schreiner Award. Baderoon had also been the winner of the Philadelphia City Paper Writing Contest in 1999 prior to the appearance of her first book.

Prolific as both an academic and a poet, Baderoon's work is deeply concerned with issues of memory and embodiment, as well as developing a language to speak about layers of gendered, racialised, buried pasts and how they shape current ways of being South African. She reports being asked several times in her first few years as a poet about why she does not write like a South African poet, to which she responded: 'I think I am a South African who writes about South African topics, but maybe I am redefining what that means to me. Maybe it means that a South African who writes about Iraq is a very normal South African, who, like most of us, thinks about the whole world'.

Zukiswa Wanner is a novelist, essayist and literary activist. She is the author of the popular novels *The Madams* (2006), *Behind Every Successful Man* (2008) and *Men of the South* (2010). She also collaborated with the late renowned photographer, Alf Khumalo, for their book *8115: A prisoner's home* in 2008. *The Madams* was shortlisted for the K Sello Duiker Award in 2007 and *Men of the South* for the 2011 Commonwealth Writer's Prize.

A big champion of writing, Wanner is a founding member of the ReadSA Initiative, a campaign to entrench reading culture among South Africans. Her work is unapologetically concerned with South African middle-class life in its many layers and messiness because this is what interests her, but also because, as she notes in a 2009 interview, 'I believe I see enough of poor stories in Africa on CNN'. Highly irritated by being reminded that popular fiction – often going by that appellation 'chick lit' – is escapist, Wanner notes that she is interested in writing that keeps readers engrossed enough to keep reading, even if some of what is on the page unsettles and shifts them from their comfort zones.

Her columns in the South African women's magazine, *True Love*, demonstrated the same pacey, witty and insightful tone that her readers have come to appreciate in her novels. The literary scholar Lynda Spencer points out that Wanner is one of a group of South African novelists who are choosing to focus shamelessly on Black femininities in ways that are not always conventional, paying attention to shifts, dilemmas and new possibilities. Although popular fiction is often dismissed as lightweight reading material, Wanner's work is characterised as 'provocative' and in her doctoral dissertation, Canadian feminist literary critic, Denise Handlarski insists that Wanner uses an accessible form to explore topics that are usually relegated to more serious, high-brow kinds of prose. Wanner comments often in interviews that what readers say to her suggests that her chosen path works towards her interests.

Finally, Xoliswa Sithole is a socialist feminist filmmaker and owner of Nayanaya Pictures. Although Sithole started out as an actor, she was deeply frustrated by the kinds of roles available to her. She had roles in *Cry Freedom* and *Mandela* before turning her hand to filmmaking because of a paucity of the kinds of exciting, vibrant women's roles she would be attracted to. As short hand, she often references that she yearned for roles in the spirit of characters like Winnie Mandela and Angela Davis. She is an independent filmmaker who values the ownership of her products, intellectual copyright aesthetically as well as politically.

Her first independent documentary film *Shouting Silent* (2002) shifted dominant discourse on child-headed households and HIV/AIDS stigma by locating herself as an AIDS orphan and granted interpretative authority to girls engaged in transactional sex and those living in areas ravaged by AIDS deaths. She returned to the topic in *Orphans of Nkandla* for which she received a British Academy Film and Television Award (BAFTA) in 2005, the first South African to do so. She received a second BAFTA in 2011 for *Zimbabwe's Forgotten Children*, a harrowing film (which she shot entirely undercover) on the effect of the Zimbabwean crisis on children's education. In 2011, this film also won her a Peabody, Canadian BANNF One World Media – Rockies Award, and the Gold Plaque at the 45th Chicago Film Festival. For Sithole, this was a very personal film since she had grown up in Zimbabwe and had been privy to some of the best education available at the time. She had started filming a different film, which is more autobiographical, about the enabling, newly independent Zimbabwe that she was raised in from three to twenty-one years of age, and in a ZANU-PF family, but that film, *Return to Zimbabwe* is still incomplete because Sithole was unable to silence her questions about contemporary Zimbabwe and focus exclusively on the film she set out to make. When she won her second BAFTA in 2011, another one of her films, *South Africa's Lost Girls,* was also nominated for the same award.

Apart from the two BAFTAs, Sithole has received the Grand Jury Prize for Best Documentary at Washington DC Independent

Film Festival (2003), 2ⁿᵈ Prize at the San Francisco Black Film Festival (2003), among others was South Africa's representative to the Nantes Film Festival (2000) and Cannes Film Festival (1999), has shown at the prestigious Pan-African Film and Television Festival of Ouagadougou (FESPACO), the Tri-Continental Film Festival, Sithengi Film Festival and various others. She insists that she makes films about women and children as a deliberate political and aesthetic choice. Sithole has also made short documentaries for various news television channels across the world. She runs the UNiTE Film Festival, which is a joint project with the United Nations, to form a film festival with a difference. UNiTE uses a different set of films by and about women to encourage dialogue during the annual 16 Days of No Violence Against Women and Children Campaign, in a format designed and copyrighted by Yanaya Communications, a division of Nayanaya Productions. Sithole is also a founder member of Filmmakers Against Racism (FAR), a group of Johannesburg-based filmmakers who responded to the 2008 eruption of xenophobic violence against working-class and poor African nationals living in Johannesburg and Cape Town. FAR declared themselves "Proudly African first, and South African second", and made a series of films, using their own resources, which were then shown in theatres, community halls and various other community spaces in order to intervene into the negrophobic violence and unsettle such feelings among South Africans. Her contribution to this project was the film *Thandeka and Martine*, and here she interrogated how women are affected by the displacement after the xenophobic outbreak. Focusing on Zimbabwean Thandeka and Congolese Martine, the film cast the spotlight on the layered gendered ways in which the crisis was experienced as well as the way in which it altered intimate relationships, parenting and senses of safety.

These are the kinds of artists that I think of as forming part of Simphiwe Dana's community in a conceptual sense. There are others and different communities that a writer can claim for her subject, some of which are suggested in the chapters that follow. I have provided some information about each of the ones I mention in class and at the beginning of this chapter deliberately. I list them in order to say something about the very important ways in which these artists differ from each other, not only because they work in different artistic mediums, but also to illustrate something about the threads running through the off-centre choices they all make. They are also attractive to me partly because of their individual eccentricities which are evident within and in addition to their art works.

I am not saying that Simphiwe Dana's renegade community is comprised only of artists, women, Black people, or only of Black women. But I have chosen to prioritise these artists for this chapter to clarify my own project here.

When I choose these particular artists to ask the question at the beginning of this chapter, it is to highlight both violence and possibility. Some of the most dangerous public messages in South Africa today are about Black girls. We are told often that they are not focused on the right things to build their future, that they are overly sexual, that they seek out sugar daddies, that they have reckless sex in order to get money from men and the State, that they are apolitical. Choosing such a list as I do here, then, I hope that my students will learn the tools to question dominance, choose to think for themselves, question whatever information is presented to them, and use these tools in order to be more than compliant citizens of the world. At the same time, it is not accidental that I have chosen to teach through creative genres, rather than choosing a Social Science discipline, which can also teach critical thinking and active citizenship as indeed all Humanities subjects are posed to do. While Social Sciences can teach critical thinking without a doubt, literary and other creative forms and their study require a double imaginative act: immersion in imaginative space in the viewing, listening and reading as well as the imaginative critical reading of the artwork as we try to understand what is at play, what matters, and what things mean.

My examples are all geniuses in creative genres. This is not an accident. They highlight quite explicitly the connections between speaking truth to power and creating alternatives. I also list artist game-changers because I want my students to think about the place of pleasure: as discovery, as disruptive and as a site of critical consciousness. This sounds counter-intuitive when expressed, but in fact, when I ask students to share what they associate these artists with, it is clear that this is not as far-fetched.

In response to any one of the named artists, inside and outside of class, even the reluctant fans or critical students say things like: 'I think she's beautiful but too intense' or 'I love her work but some of it makes me uncomfortable' or 'I disagree with the content of her work, but she makes me think' or 'I don't like her work at all because she is so serious' or even 'I love her work, but I wish she'd make a happy film next time'. They know the work and feel strongly about it one way or another. Some students express more appreciative words of the artists.

It seems, then, that what these young people are saying is that these are women whose artworks and public presences make audiences think at the same time as they create products that are enjoyable. This is so much more than the bizarre South African obsession with 'art that has a message', which is only *partly* an inheritance from art for political ends. These are artists who are able to do something important in an age of celebrity culture where personalities are often famous for their capacity for self-promotion much more than for any particular capacity. Celebrity culture, as Thato Mapule shows, is often premised on the worship of the prominent figure in ways that are also at the same time linked to consumption. We cannot think about celebrity culture outside of the age of late capitalist consumerism. Fame meant something else a thousand years ago than it does now. It also required a different engagement. Mapule writes:

The preoccupation with famous individuals and stardom has its historical roots in the social fixation with monarchical subjects such as kings, queens and emperors. The status of these elite subjects was ascribed through lineage and blood line (Rojek 2001; Evans and Hesmondalgh 2007). Braudy's (1987: 268) focus on Alexander the Great is useful in tracing the historical idealisation of fame and the emergence of charismatic authority as a central theme in conceptualising stardom and celebrity. The charismatic quality of these ascribed celebrities also distinguished them from ordinary individuals. These inherent talents were understood as a gift of nature or as god-given and could not, therefore, be explained rationally. The talents of ascribed celebrities represented the ideals that the untalented and ordinary individual could only dream of emulating and made such celebrated persons worthy of public admiration (Weber 2007:17–24; Dyer 1991: 57–60).

However, with the advent of democracy and capitalism, stardom has been democratised, giving way to a more utilitarian conception of stardom: celebrity (Turner 2004: 89). The notion of the utilitarian nature of celebrity was conceived of in Greek mythology, where the term 'celebrity' denoted to the fall of the gods and the rise of democratic governments and secular society. The Grecian conception of celebrity appears somewhat ironic when applied to the modern view of the term, as today's famous persons do not possess royal or elitist lineage, but are ordinary individuals who have come to be treated like gods and are celebrated by many (Rojek 2001: 11).

In other words, as Mapule argues, the older model of fame applied to people seen as exceptional because they were born into that realm (royalty) or achieved such status (athletes or warriors). Such figures invited public admiration. They were seen as the polar opposite of what it meant to be ordinarily human. At the same time, Mapule shows that the more useful notions of celebrity are also not brand new because Greek mythology already possessed aspects of the famous as ordinary people who achieve celebrity.

Today, the definition of celebrity is much closer to being seen and manufactured. In her own words:

Celebrities are defined as public individuals who are held in great esteem in society because of their ubiquitous appearance within the media. The repetitive appearance of celebrities accrues these individuals' discursive power in society over ordinary individuals... Unlike other famous persons within the history of fame, the modern celebrity lacks any talent or special achievement, but is deemed important because of their omnipresence within the mediums of print and broadcasting.

Something about Simphiwe Dana and the other artists I discuss above will not fit into this model of celebrity. Something about these women means they are able to retain a grasp of the collective imagination – whether creatively or sparking negativity – at the same time that they stand out. In other words, they can be on the cover of women's magazines, have meals interrupted by fans who want to take photographs and request autographs, on the one hand, but they also have something that is very specific about them that even when copied does not transmit properly.

I don't mean substance. All human beings have substance, whether they let it show or not.

There is clearly a book in there somewhere about how artists like these, who are both incredibly talented and so unlike any other artist of their time, are able to negotiate the kinds of presence that these women have. This is not that book, although people interested in the minutiae of how to build brands would benefit from *that* book.

There is also no doubt much to be learnt about details of these artists' own lives, and I look forward to reading biographies on all of them. If you picked up this book hoping to find a lot of details of Simphiwe's private life, you will be somewhat disappointed because where there are private details of her life, I do not use them in the same kind of way as her biographer might find them useful.

What I am interested in here is thinking about Simphiwe out loud. I have many questions that have continued to plague me about her role and place in South African society. I have been fascinated by both what she achieves and what she elicits. On the one hand, she is utterly adored by many as her awards, reviews, sales and audience responses show. On the other, she is constantly told that she does not know her place.

Why is it so important for her to know her place?

What is this place?

And why is there only one appropriate one?

Even more importantly, why do those who attempt to remind her of her waywardness feel compelled to point this out since it clearly contrasts with her own sense of what her places are?

As a human being, she is full of contradictions. But she lives some of hers in the public glare without seeming to experience any real crisis. That there are people who want to see her brought down a notch every now and again is nothing special – even if it must be hurtful. Thato Mapule reminds us that a central aspect of celebrity culture is the adoration of famous people that is always haunted by the desire for their downfall. In other words, we want celebrities to be like gods and goddesses that we constantly look up to and stalk. Yet we want them to fall to confirm that they are mere mortals, like us. It is not just *Schadenfreude*, therefore, that led to the mean-spirited tweeting after *Sunday Sun* revealed details of Simphiwe's relationship with a married former kwaito musician in 2013. As Grace Musila pointed out in private correspondence with me over this book, this duality in celebrity culture is also reminiscent of older Greek tragic theatre. In such theatre 'man unlimited' is celebrated as the embodiment of the greatest human accomplishment, on the one hand. On the other hand, 'man limited' is also welcomed as it shows the flaws of the gods/goddesses, thereby bringing them to the level of the ordinary human.

These women whose names I list provide some of the context through which I discuss Simphiwe Dana's relevance in South Africa today. By this, I do not mean that Dana is the kind of woman that the above are, although this would be difficult to show too, given how different all of these women are among themselves. At the

same time, as individual as Simphiwe is, she ...
where women who are daringly ground-breaking ...
chosen life are possible. This is one of South Africa's ...
because it also makes such women possible.

When I note that these are the women who form the co...
that Simphiwe Dana is part of, I do not mean friendships, alt...
some of these exist. There are also marked ways in which Simph.we
is different from the women I mention above. All the others are very
unapologetic feminists. Simphiwe has a more fluid relationship
with feminism, as I discuss in more detail in 'Desiring Simphiwe
2: The soft feminist', later in this book. We know more about her
private life because she sometimes speaks about it in interviews,
revealing much more often than the others. Yet, as a mother, some
of her decisions to keep her two children out of the spotlight are
very similar to those adopted by Mashile and Mazwai.

Simphiwe Dana is one of a generation of creatives who have
emerged with such a brilliant signature that they have presented
a model scarcely seen before. I am fascinated by these artists and
their art. It is important that many come from places that 'celebrity'
does not ordinarily come from, or that they conduct themselves in
ways less afraid of the implications of their political power.

One of the reasons I think Simphiwe Dana is so captivating is
because she troubles many categories of belonging in the South
African public imagination in the most remarkable ways. By public
imagination, I mean the collective language we adopt and see
reflected in the press, in popular culture, in political rhetoric, on
the letters' pages, that is repeated in what callers who comment on
talk radio shows say. In some respects, it is the received wisdom.
It is not that there is only one way of thinking in South Africa or
that the public imagination is coherent and thinks consistently in
the same way.

At the same time, there are some things that are more
specifically in line with the spirit of the time. I could use language
that mentions people like Jürgen Habermas's public sphere, or
Raymond Williams's structures of feelings. And indeed, what I
have in mind is linked to, and has aspects of, these conceptions

or *zeitgeist*. All of them attempt to describe something about the spirit of a time: a collectively recognised set of values, assumptions and meanings that becomes a visible truth and is contested in a specific place. They become a truth because they are repeated so much that we find ourselves believing them to be 'normal' and we use them to navigate our lives without even thinking about them. They all pop to the surface when specific topics are explicitly discussed; they lie unspoken but influential the rest of the time.

This is why Simphiwe is both so passionately adored and needs to be taken down a notch in the public's eye, to varying ends, as I discuss in the chapter 'Uncontained: Simphiwe's Africa'. Most people want to analyse Ms Dana's public exchange with the Premier of South Africa's Western Cape Province, Helen Zille as a moment on its own to make sense of it. Such an exercise makes sense, but when analysed alongside other moments of public critique more is clarified about Simphiwe Dana and South Africa's failure to engage the imagination fully, especially within the public sphere.

I met varied responses when I mentioned that I am writing this book. Some of these comments perfectly resonated with Simphiwe's place in the public imagination. Some people insisted that a biography on her would be more interesting than anything else. To these, I suggested that there is room to write more than one kind of book concerned with Simphiwe. A few people suggested that there was biography overload in South Africa right now. But most people with whom I had any kind of conversation about the book were quite happy to imagine the kind of book that they wanted this to be, unmoored to what I had in mind. I was tickled by this somewhat.

This, then, is a book that responds to the very significant invitation to the courage and imagination that Simphiwe Dana issues. In it I scrutinise the many ways in which her public work offers us an opportunity to collectively shift our senses of what is possible. I am convinced that both the content of her work – her lyrics, her acting, her columns, her blogs – and our varied responses to her, show us something about where such a shift is needed. Her vision is daring and prophetic, and this explains many public responses to her. She has her finger on several pulses even if we are not always listening to her on the requisite frequency.

We come from people who for millennia knew that art is the site of wisdom, even though we now pretend otherwise. There is wisdom in Simphiwe's work. There is also invitation and inspiration. She is a human being, so there is also evidence of where she has not yet come to terms with her own wisdom. This is not reason to postpone this response. This book, then, tries to amplify aspects of Simphiwe's public life and significance.

Some of what she points to needs urgent hearing, but prophets are often unheard in their own time. At the same time, her profundity is not only in her prophetic vision. There is much freedom for our individual selves if we allow ourselves some of the permissions she wrestles with.

CHAPTER 2

Rapport

Natalia Molebatsi and Raphael d'Abdon note that Simphiwe Dana's first two albums are 'spiritual and political offerings conceived in IsiXhosa and laid out on a jazz background'.

When I came across this description recently, I was delighted because, although they published this journal article in which they make this evaluation long before I started writing this book, I read it in the days approaching the deadline for *A Renegade Called Simphiwe*. Molebatsi and d'Abdon's article is not on Dana, but on poetry, so this gem of a line was hidden somewhere in an academic article that I was reading for other purposes. These writers' sense of Simphiwe's work as spiritual, political and musically vibrant has synergies with how I write about Simphiwe in the book you hold in your hands, and with what prompted me to write *A Renegade Called Simphiwe*.

And now, let me start again as intended by going back to Simphiwe's December 2010 concert. The tickets were my birthday present to myself.

At the concert that doubled as Simphiwe Dana's DVD recording, my then life partner and I sat next to a young man who was as entranced as I was by Simphiwe's music, magic and performance presence. It was a sold out concert at the Lyric Theatre at Gold Reef City, in Johannesburg; full of people who clearly appreciate her music. Whether she was singing from her first album, *Zandisile*, the then still newish third album *Kulture Noir*, or the supposedly unpopular second offering, *The One Love Movement on Bantu Biko Street*, Ms Dana had her audience eating out of her hand and singing along to every lyric. The mood in that room was not just the frenzied air of a music concert, intoxicatingly delicious though that atmosphere often is. This was prime Simphiwe Dana: resplendent. Dana has always loved performing live, and it seemed she had never loved it as much as she did that night.

Because of this ambiance I was not surprised when the young man in the seat next to me prodded me, in the camaraderie that often develops at such places of collective joy, to share the thoughts he could not save until later, for someone he had a real intimacy with.

'Some people go to Church. Other people came to this concert', he shouted in my ear.

He didn't know me.

I could have been a religious fanatic who would be offended by the blasphemy in his words.

We would walk right past each other without a second glance as strangers if we had a chance encounter today. But that evening we were part of the same community. He took a leap of faith and assumed that I would understand what he meant in the spirit with which he meant it: to say something about Simphiwe Dana's extraordinary gift, not to take anything away from God.

I think he was also saying something about how Dana's genius is her gift to our interior selves. What she sang about affirmed deep, dark places within ourselves that are always part of us, but that very often remain unloved and unspoken, or worse: disowned and unspeakable. When she sings '*Ndim lo, ndim iqhawe! Iqhaw' elonzakeleyo*', she partly speaks to these inner selves that we leave hidden even from ourselves. These lyrics that translate into literally 'Here I am, I am heroic, a wounded hero' or more concisely: 'Here I stand, wounded hero' resonate and offer so many possibilities for healing that might otherwise fester into that which kills us, physically and spiritually. This entire song, the third track from her third album, offers both the recognition of wounding and the possibility of healing. But in the poignant lyrics lies an invitation to think with a new vocabulary. We have to use language differently. We have to think about what we stand for differently. The power of this song also comes from how Simphiwe sings it. The emotional transportation that the young man speaks about is also influenced by its singer's ability to offer the lyrics in a voice that blends strength and vulnerability.

In South African culture, we often use heroism and heroic masculinity as though they mean the same thing, as though this is the only possible demonstration of courage worth celebrating, or as though it is the most important. Simphiwe suggests in this song that we need to think counter-intuitively about courage, and about who we call 'qhawe'. Thandiswa Mazwai throws the gauntlet in a very linked project on her song 'Nizalwa Ngobani?', from Zabalaza (2004), where she puts women in the centre of thinking about heroism. What these songs ask us to think about is heroism in relation to ourselves, in relation to what requires courage to live in the world today. In these songs of these geniuses, 'qhawe' is not an easy category to identify. Simphiwe insists that she is a hero, and when we sing along, individually we assert the same that we too are the wounded heroic.

What kind of heroism are we now called upon to embrace here?

What does it mean to think about ourselves, our survival as heroic and therefore worthy of recognition at the same time that we attend to our woundedness?

More than one reading of wounded heroism is possible. For those who take for granted that all human beings are wounded in one way or another, such a juxtaposition of vulnerability and courage is refreshing. It can even be counter-intuitive.

When we pay attention to the larger context of the song, the album and recurrent preoccupations with African senses of self and healing, with new meanings of Blackness, the wound Simphiwe's song refers to is colonial wounding. It is collective African memory of occupation, displacement and defeat. The colonial wound is also linked to the deferment of freedom psychically and materially.

In Mazwai's song, the historic heroic community fights against colonialism as she lists various anti-colonial and anti-apartheid visionaries. For Mazwai, there is a current wilful forgetting of this heroic legacy that needs urgent address, as is evident in the rebuke '*Nizilibel' u'ba nizalwa ngobani*' which translates equally into 'Have you forgotten who you come from?' and 'You have forgotten whose children you are'. The ambiguity about whether this is a statement of disapproval or a challenging question is itself productive because Mazwai's voice lists the courageous fighters, with each mention punctuated with '*qhawe lama qhawe*' (hero of the heroic). At the same time, bravery also contains the wilful remembering of the heroic wounded often left outside of the narrative of heroic masculinity. Therefore, where Simphiwe Dana offers herself as wounded heroic figure who will change the future and destroy metaphoric mountains, Thandiswa Mazwai insists on a historic heroic community that has been let down by the living collective 'you'. The two songs are conceptually linked, even if at first glance they seem to relate to the temporal continuum of heroism differently, with Thandiswa's lyrics glancing backwards for inspiration, and Simphiwe's forward looking. For Thandiswa, responding to a rich courageous past also requires expanding the very languaging of anti-racist struggle. Whereas '*qhawe*' *ngesiXhosa* applies to brave people of any gender, the artist chooses '*ukuzalwa*', a feminine metaphor ('birthing') to denote this lineage. That Belede, her own activist mother's name (but not necessarily her father's) is included in the list, as well as the repetition of Madikizela (for Winnie Madikizela Mandela) further underscores the deliberate gendered inflection of Ms Mazwai's project. Both Madikizela and Belede are named unambiguously, one through her first name and the latter through her birth family name, rather than the one she used for most of her activist life, but which, because she shares with her equally famous husband, is often assumed to refer to him. Winnie Mandela may have had a much longer activist life than her husband, Nelson, but patriarchally 'Mandela' is assumed to refer to him, not her.

The two engagements with heroism by Thandiswa Mazwai and Simphiwe Dana are not mutually exclusive, even if they differently stretch the imagination of how to respond heroically in the present.

For Simphiwe's song, if we are to change things, we need to pay attention to both our extreme courage and our wound – at the same time. We need to claim both. '*Ndim lo*' is an assertion of presence; it is much more than mere identification. It is not like putting your hand up in class and saying 'present, Miss'. It is much more like standing, with chest out and chin up, confidently claiming space. If heroes change things, they do so through embattlement. Wounds result and they become part of claiming self. This has so many implications for what we have survived and the courage we have to create more change through the hardship.

This turning inward resonates with her declaration at this concert that the opening song was a prayer of sorts. She reminded us that there was prayer in Africa before the dominant monotheistic forms of religion that exist now. This statement is less about these latter religions and more about feeling connected to the universe, where the interior always matters.

She was saying our inner lives matter and deserve attention and love. It is an invitation to turn inward, to pay attention. Simphiwe is saying here, as she does again and again in her music, what is inside matters – all of it. Our feelings, our hurt, our joys, our pleasure and our fears matter. She invites us to turn inward as part of changing the world. And she says so not in the language of 'manifesting our dreams' that is so dominant in our world today, where we can change the world by simply imagining ourselves differently and leaving it at that.

No.

What Simphiwe was saying at that concert is in sync with what she sang about in her first, second and third albums. It is all over the album that she is in the process of making as I write this. It is not a gimmick. Her call and invitation, whilst we are entranced by the sheer splendour of her voice, is to choose ourselves. For Simphiwe our interior matters. By interior, here, I refer to any of the following as well as the collective co-existence of all of the following: our imagination, our fears, our pain, our thoughts, our feelings, our spiritual bearings. In other words, when I speak about the interior I mean the psychological, the spiritual, the mental and the imagination all together. I repeat this because in conversations about interiority, I am often reminded by Social Scientists that I have left out the imagination. I have not. I begin with the imagination.

Simphiwe says it all matters. What is important to us matters. We matter. How we feel and think and desire matters. Black Consciousness Movement (BCM) leader, Steve Biko and his comrades said so too. They said what we call ourselves, how we see ourselves and others like us, our senses of our entitlement in the world, what we deem possible, what gives us joy, what wounds us, our experience, matter. For the activists of that movement it was important that Black was neither the same as 'non-white' nor a given identity based solely on your body. To identify as Black was both a deliberate public political stance and a statement of a frame of mind. It was both. You could move from 'non-white' to Black only once you chose 'psychological liberation', which encompassed your feelings about yourself, other Black people, Blackness as well as white supremacy. There is consistency on this in Biko's own writing as Frank Talk and in the collection *I Write what I Like*, the collective writing by BCM activists in various BCM publications such as *Black Review*, the reports of the various community programmes and the creative arts this movement inspired. Psychological liberation was crucial for the Black unity that would successfully end apartheid and all white supremacy. But even a cursory engagement with the ideological sites of this movement (Black Pride, Black Beauty, Black Theology, Black Arts, Black History) highlights the insistence on coupling interiority with materiality.

Feminism also places emphasis on the interior world as important, where emotions and experience are worthy sites of knowledge in and of themselves. This lies at the heart of many feminist strands' insistence on theorising from women's lived realities.

Paying attention to interior worlds is an important part of how we change. It is not indulgence. The revolutionary feminist lesbian

Audre Lorde reminded us that self-care is revolutionary work: 'Caring for myself is not self-indulgence, it is self-preservation, and that is an act of political warfare.'

There was something transformative about that Lyric Theatre concert. There was the possibility of a transformation that brings us closer to ourselves in her music more broadly. This is part of what the young man sitting next to me did not need to spend time explaining. He was not necessarily thinking about Biko and Lorde when he spoke. Nonetheless, he recognised the meeting places of pleasure and attention to the interior as transformative.

I smiled and agreed.

This was not the first time I had seen Simphiwe perform. While there had never been any doubt of her talent or presence, there had been significant growth in her stage performance. In earlier concerts she was playful, witty and sweet; she had now come into a different kind of power, a new buoyancy.

In an interview with Simphiwe in the South African women's magazine, *True Love*, Thando Pato compares Simphiwe earlier in her career and the artist after her second album, noticing that the older Simphiwe is a woman who now more obviously embraces joy and the ordinary pleasures of life.

When she had entered the dark stage at the beginning of her show, she had declared '*Ndinedyudyu*'. We were all momentarily sucked in by this declaration of extreme nervousness, perhaps even missing how carefully she chose the coy, intimate form of the noun to use with this audience. She has used '*idyudyu*' not '*ukoyika*' or '*uvalo*'. Declarations of anxiety notwithstanding, the Dana performing that night was an artist that had come into her own, inhabiting her skin in a more confident grown-up manner than the young woman who knew from her very first performances that she was ready to fly and needed only the space and air. She had then, early in her career, told us this in as many words in '*Ndiredi*' from her first album, *Zandisile*. Now we were seeing what she was ready for.

This vulnerability was a very different face to the ones she presents when she is writing opinion editorials on race, language

26

and education in contemporary South African national weekly newspapers. Thando Pato admitted to being surprised when encountering 'young and energetic' Simphiwe at her second interview with the artist. Pato admits to nervously expecting a Simphiwe from before whose 'head wraps constantly covered her hair', but instead finding herself faced with Simphiwe's youthfulness and vulnerability. In her July 2007 cover piece for *True Love* magazine, Pato would write:

> The first time I interviewed Simphiwe Dana, it was just after the release of her first album, Zandisile, in 2004... My impression of her at the time was that she was very guarded, very serious and had a heavy energy about her. But a lot has happened since then. Simphiwe is now celebrating the success of her second album, One Love Movement on Bantu Biko Street, which won her four SAMAs this year, and she is preparing for a two month tour of Europe.

In what follows, Simphiwe shows how keenly aware she is of these two capacities within: the deep, serious side as well as the side that seeks to be 'ordinary'. Pressed by Pato to speak about how she can be 'ordinary', Simphiwe notes:

> I'm ordinary in my own way and it works for me. What I am saying is that I don't have to worry about things all the time. I just want to be an ordinary girl and have fun. You know, dance, make jokes and talk about nothing. Why do we always have to talk about something all the time? Why can't we just talk about pink, you know what I am saying?

She credits her facial scar and survival from a harrowing accident with this new youthfulness and commitment to live out fully in all her capacities: to speak plainly, to work hard, to enjoy life and to take it seriously at the same time. She chose to keep the scar after the accident and was struck both by how close danger always is, and how magical survival can be. She continues:

27

[The accident] made me realise there has to be a balance – you work hard but you have to play.

My music is a very heavy, deep side of me and when I'm there I'm not like this. I'm very depressed when the music comes out and I don't have to live there all the time. And this [the scar] made me realise that I don't have to carry the depression all the time. I can put it down and be this carefree person to survive this journey that I am on. So now I play and my kids are so happy. I'm happy. I go out, have fun and come back and dance with my kids. I like my life a lot.

In other words, then, both sides of Simphiwe are present and indeed it is possible to see them feeding off each other. The serious Simphiwe is as evident in her public writing as the gentle Simphiwe who takes life seriously and assumes that all human beings have the capacity – and entitlement – to enjoy being ordinary. In using her critical voice, we see Simphiwe Dana's substantial mind working in her capacity as a public intellectual, even though this label is so maligned in South Africa today.

People who love her music for whatever reason often battle to come to terms with this other side to Ms Dana's persona. They are happy to dance to her music, to be tickled, affirmed or provoked by her lyrics, but they sometimes resist being challenged in their thinking by the same person. There are many reasons for this, as far as I can see. There are probably many more that I cannot see yet.

What is clear is that Simphiwe Dana, magical-voiced musician, is a woman who will not be prevented from speaking her mind on some of the most important issues of her day. And she will do so and continue to remind us of the value of turning inward, even if it is not possible to always do so. She is an artist, not a pamphleteer. Joy and politics are intertwined but because *how* we hear differs from moment to moment and among listeners, we sometimes need the pleasurable aspects of her music more than the politics, and vice versa. We always get both. But we choose what to foreground depending on what we need and desire at the time.

She often tells us to step away from our comfort zones. Sometimes she entices us to do so. At other times, she yanks us out. Our responses vary, but Simphiwe's invitation is consistent. Her vision is steady, which is not the same thing as predictable. Whether we like it or not, she challenges us to think differently from the familiar, to choose heroic imagination and embrace possibility. We love and reject her for this.

Some people argue that this is in line with how artists are positioned historically in African societies – that they provoke critical thinking through both their craft and by being uncontained in their criticism of whosoever invites their ire. In this framework, even when you disagree with Simphiwe Dana's public utterances or writings, she is not doing anything strange by speaking her mind. These people like to locate her within the tradition of *griots*, and this makes sense too.

Others see this resolve to speak her mind on things non-musical as overstepping the boundaries of acceptability. This latter group thinks celebrated musicians should 'stick to what they do best', by which they mean making music. They should leave politics, policy, identity and the larger cultural terrain to other kinds of professionals. Such sentiment is often expressed not just in relation to Simphiwe Dana, but in response to other creative types when they speak in genres other than the ones they have become prominent for. People who try to make Dana 'stay in her place', steer clear of political matters and simply write music, are clearly not paying any attention to the content of her music. They may be dancing to the entrancing '*Ilolo*', but they are not hearing her unwavering commitment in those very lyrics to speak her truth regardless. They may sing '*Ndikhangela igama lam*', but they do not pause to ask themselves what it really means to 'look for our own name'. They also have clearly never heard of Miriam Makeba, Nina Simone, Angelique Kidjo, Queen Latifah or Meshell Ndegeocello. These are artists with divergent politics, and each has been as talented as she has been politically hard to contain.

But Simphiwe Dana's place in post-apartheid South Africa is further complicated by the fact that she also seems to present contradictions to how public women should behave. She speaks forcefully on the politics of language, education and race. In a country where women are constantly pressurised to exert feminine power, she can be hard to make sense of or live with.

How can an artist who makes us feel so good about ourselves through her music also take us on so abrasively in her public writing?

What we really mean when we ask this question is: how *dare* she?

How dare she use that space we have opened up to her to make us face our linguistic shame?

Who does she think she is, making it so difficult for us dismiss her as either reactionary or state apologist?

And as if this is not complicated enough, Dana's romantic life – or at least its public face – rubs up against other aspects of our collective identities and spaces of denial we do not want to deal with. Here again, she will not stay in place. She tweets about the importance of monogamy and fidelity, and holds marriage in high esteem. But then one Sunday, South Africa wakes up to allegations in both the mainstream and the tabloid press about shenanigans that contradict her tweets on relationships. How can she be in a relationship with a married man? Is her business partner her lover, her friend or her patron? Are these three contradictory?

The responses to these revelations in the press were quite telling, not so much on Simphiwe Dana as an individual, but of her place in the public imagination in our country. Infidelity is commonplace in South Africa. This suggests that there was more going on with responses to Dana's love life, captured quite aggressively on Twitter and other public sentiments, than mere concern over marital infidelity. And in a country where the discussion on same-sex desire and love is so inconsistent, and where accusations of being a lesbian often mark a woman as safe for public scorn and violence (as we saw in speculation on the sexual orientation of national women's football team *Banyana Banyana* players a few years ago), what did it mean for Ms Dana to be marked as a possible lesbian?

What are we to make, too, of Simphiwe's ability to demonstrate such control over her public and private life that, until recently, she was almost entirely without scandal and her publicity machine worked like a well-oiled vehicle, on the one hand, and the SMS published in the press as her responses to questions about her love and sex life? These text messages which suggest that she feels both torn and remorseful, and her immediate response to the scandal upon her return to Twitter, seem to suggest a naïveté that is out of step with her career thus far. Had she been a more calculating human being, it might be easy to simply assume that this is savvy use of publicity. The glib within public relations circles argue that no press is bad press. However, witnessing her deep agony over the entire saga, not just the public face of it all, requires a different line of considerations.

Responses to her albums are also quite telling. She has mentioned in various interviews that she often feels unappreciated as an artist in South Africa. The same public that adores her for *Zandisile* and *Kulture Noir* chooses to distance itself from *One Love Movement on Bantu Biko Street*. Even Bongani Madondo, one of our most perceptive cultural critics and writers, wrote a response to Dana's second album that suggested that he would not engage it, even as it contained material akin to the kind of content he usually produces incisive copy on.

Simphiwe Dana is able to occupy a range of places in South Africa's imagination that do not always make sense alongside one another. She forces us to think and exist in ways that we may not otherwise choose. She will not stay in place and we are not sure what to make of what appear to be contradictions in her public persona. She makes us uncomfortable sometimes because she makes us feel too much.

This is power. She refuses containment. Simphiwe Dana is a renegade.

She is hard to pin down and lock into one box. In one sense this is human. In another sense, she challenges even the boundaries of rebellion. South African publics love her and eat out of her hand. But they can also be enraged by her.

Think about the Western Cape Premier's response to Dana's

ongoing critique of Capetonian structural racism. Premier Zille's rebuttals surface admiration of Dana's music alongside an attempt to correct the artist's position on politics. It is a suggestion that Dana should do something slightly different than what she has chosen to do. I return to this incident in more detail later.

This book is one writer's engagement with the Simphiwe Dana of the South African public imagination. I am convinced that she matters in a range of ways and I am concerned here with what her 'rebel' status shows us about her and about ourselves, collectively, when you pay attention to how we respond to her. If she really is a prophetess ahead of her time and therefore unappreciated in her village, I think we had better pay attention. Appreciation is not the same thing as blind adoration.

I am not satisfied with readings of her as contradictory, or even more harshly, as hypocritical. While a famous writer told me she thinks Simphiwe is quite conventionally feminine, I argue here that she is a renegade.

Although this book is not a biography, I look forward to various biographies on Simphiwe. I also look forward to other kinds of books on her: books by people with a more intimate knowledge of the depth of musical innovation that characterises her *oeuvre*, studies on her poetic lyrics and a coffee table book on her consummate style. I cannot wait to press 'play' from my couch as I watch the first documentary on her. I think she matters *that* much.

In this book, I do not discuss things to do with her children. She has not asked this, but she lives it. As a parent myself, I understand the desire to protect one's children from a public life not of their choosing.

Even as friends, we disagree on many things, some of which will be very obvious in this book. We have had very heated arguments in private and on Twitter. As incredibly gentle and generous as Simphiwe is, she can be very stubborn. She would say I can be quite impossible. Maybe we are both right. She has had access to two drafts of the book, and will read this book once it is finished, but she has known about it, and apart from a brief comment or two in which she expressed curiosity, she has not directly probed its contents.

The first time I told her I was writing it, she said 'I don't really understand what you're going to write, but you're a writer, so go ahead. It's your book'.

Laughing, I offered, 'I wasn't asking for your permission, I was just telling you.'

Also laughing, she replied, 'I wasn't offering my consent. *Ubuzayithini*? (What would you need it for)?'

I wanted to take on this project as part of a conversation with her, with fellow human beings at this time. Obviously, what I focus on is what interests, bothers, delights or haunts me. I think renegades are important – and I think renegade artists are especially instructive. I could have written this book as an academic study, and so some of the analysis borrows tools from my writing in the academy. But it is not a scholarly text. I bring to it both my intellectual and creative writing selves because that is what this subject has demanded from my spirit.

Why Simphiwe?

Because this is what she invites by owning herself in the way that she does.

Because I think it is important to write the kinds of books we would like to read and I have often valued other writer's works even though they were not written for me. I have wanted to read a book like this on her, on Thandiswa Mazwai, on other artists I find artistically magical. I *will* write a different kind of book on Ms Mazwai even though thinking about it frightens me.

I can't write all the books I would love to read. I can barely read all the books I buy. But I have chosen to write this one.

I am fascinated by genius and by rebels. Renegades have so much to teach us about humanity. We really need to rethink the place of the creative in South Africa right now and start to pay attention to art in radically different ways than we have done recently. The life of an artist and the many ways in which she 'presses South Africa's buttons' is one way to show the importance of responding to the gift of artistic genius we have so much of at this time. It is a huge missed opportunity to respond to this courageous imaginative invitation with the pretence that art and artists are simply here for our entertainment, and that entertainment only means escape.

Before I turn to the rest of the book, let me clarify a few things about some of my choices. I have referred to many of her songs, the 'spirit' of such songs or the gist of these songs when I have been analysing her writing, statements and behaviour beyond the musical stage. This is because I think these are intertwined and because I think different aspects of her life, pronouncements and creative production give us insight into her.

I have sometimes translated parts of her lyrics and referred to other parts without quoting them. No translation is ever exact, so I have sometimes translated the same lyrics in more than one way. This is not because I am trying to fight the inevitable loss that haunts all translation, a futile exercise in any event. It is rather because there are specific inflections of the lyrics' many meanings that I want to stress at that time. I know that some meaning escapes even attempts to dissect and discuss it, another inevitability that I find freeing rather than frustrating.

Language is such fraught terrain at another level: which language? Why translate? There are so many assumptions and anxieties about audiences that haunt every decision about language. Simphiwe offers such refreshing possibilities for how we think about our relationships to language as African peoples. I discuss this in much more detail in the chapter 'Love, language and anguish'.

There is a reason that there are two chapters called 'Desiring Simphiwe'. I had initially imagined that they would form part of the same chapter and I would play with the pun in ways that allowed me to join them. The chapter would juxtapose Simphiwe as desired (other people desiring Simphiwe) and what Simphiwe reveals about her desires (Simphiwe desiring X). But then each section became so long, it was clear that I was forcing matters in trying to keep them as a single entity, when they were in fact Siamese twins.

I have written this book so that you can read the chapters in any order you wish. I do hope that you read the first two chapters first. But you do not need to read it in the order in which the chapters appear. The chapters are self-contained and connected to each other at the same time, but they do not build on each other in a linear fashion. If you wish, you can treat it like your CDs: read one chapter and then another back to front. Read a chapter today and another next month. Or you can read all of them as they appear or in random order. This ordering is just my personal preference.

Finally, this is not a biography, although it does have biographical aspects within the broad spectrum of creative non-fiction. I call it a portrait in words. Parts of it are clearly an intellectual biography. When you release your words into the world, it is not so important to keep tight reigns on what they are called. So, I will hand that one over. As Ingrid Masondo says about her photographs in one of the epigraphs to this book, blurriness offers us the possibility to see differently, tilt our heads, squint and think for ourselves at the same time that we are in conversation with what is in front of us. Well, that is not what she really says. But it *is* also what she is saying. Isn't it?

CHAPTER 3

Desiring Simphiwe 1:
An artist's shadows

I want to start this chapter by telling a quick story.

When I became single after a long-term civil life partnership with a Black artist-intellectual, two strange things unexpectedly brought Simphiwe Dana into my conversational life. They did not so much happen to me as draw me into their weirdness. In separate encounters with two Black intellectual men, whom I will call Zuko and Donald, over a period of less than a month, Simphiwe Dana's name was casually dropped as someone they each may have had a romantic encounter with. Her name came up again in a third encounter with another man, Malik, somewhat similarly placed, but he did not claim to be her ex. He mentioned her as an example of a certain type of femininity in a conversation that actually was about masculinities and femininities. I mention Malik in this chapter because part of this third conversation helped me make sense of what was going on with the two earlier ones, which I did not discuss with him.

I was as struck by Zuko's and Donald's revelations of previous dalliance with Simphiwe as I was by the suggestion that I might be interested in knowing about such a past. While listening to these stories, several things went through my mind. I was aware that what I was being told may or may not be true. Even as I listened to these men temporarily, I was more interested in why they were telling me this than I was in whether they were, in fact, telling the truth. I was also somewhat disappointed to witness two adult men carelessly reveal aspects of their previous lives that were, in fact, not just theirs to tell. What did it mean for them to reveal details of a famous woman's private life to someone they were differently flirting with?

Both alleged former lovers dropped her name and this sense of her in conversations that were not about her or music. No other information was offered by these men of other previous relationships at the same time or later, in the same manner. Before these conversations, only Zuko knew that I knew Simphiwe socially.

Zuko and Donald put up very interesting performances, yet both were at pains to convince me that these revelations were unplanned. Neither one of them really understood the distance between persistence and aggression. Zuko emphasised that he had chosen to declare his dalliance with Simphiwe against his better judgement because he does not ordinarily 'kiss and tell' and therefore does not want to appear to be 'that kind of man'. It was very difficult to take this reluctance seriously considering he has just volunteered the details of 'a past lover' unprovoked and not connected to anything we had been discussing prior to that point. Zuko was at pains to assure me that this declaration is totally different from such immature and inappropriate behaviour, adding that he was very nervous as he told me because he had rendered himself so vulnerable in front of me. Secondly, he informed me, because he knows some women are not likely to have a relationship with a friend's former flame, telling me about his past with Simphiwe was a big risk for him given the fact that I may choose to reject him on this basis.

What I know is that when people insist on telling you how deep, progressive and profound they are, rather than showing you, they are trying to manipulate you. The late radical feminist

Andrea Dworkin, who always had such delicious turn of phrase, once said, 'it is not terrifically important to us that [men] learn to cry; it is important to us that they stop the crimes of violence against us'. As I listened to Zuko, I remixed Dworkin's phrase to 'it is not terrifically important to me that men tell me how proto-feminist and sensitive they are, it is important that they be feminist men'. I was not really impressed by this performance of sensitive masculinity. None of the feminist men in my life have ever had to tell me to see how beautiful, feminist and sensitive they are. I am perfectly capable of interpreting what I see for myself.

The first time I encountered this mating dance, I was amused by the farce. I read between the lines for a living. The second time, I was taken aback because I immediately remembered the former event of a similar kind. I was now very curious.

This time, Donald started out telling me there had been a rumour about Simphiwe and him. I bit my tongue to stop from adding 'that you and your friends started'. The smile on his face as he told this story made me wonder how long he had carried this torch for Simphiwe. He then proceeded to tell me, 'in confidence', about how the rumour had been true. I asked him why he was telling me and whether he did not think he was a little too old for this kind of behaviour. He may have been genuinely discomfited by my questions and the absence of awe in my voice. I was not paying sufficient attention by that stage. This distancing was the only way to keep my irritation in perspective.

I was not convinced by any of the performances of these men. This was a very specific mating dance that both of them were pulling me into. The dance incorporated the carefully executed moves that included feigned anxiety and false casualness. The revelations were as innocent as natural make-up and just-out-of-bed hair. Although the latter is a very messy, sexy, tussled look that women with straight hair can pull off that makes them look like they just jumped out of bed, it is, in fact, a very cultivated look. The former requires carefully applied make-up so that the wearer appears make-up free to the ordinary eye. These two men were not that slick.

Simphiwe Dana clearly stands for something very similar in Zuko's and Donald's imaginations. This is obviously not a coordinated effort by the two of them, so I am not arguing for a conspiracy theory here. I have also not seen this particular projection of her in the public before, so if these men are pointing to some sense of Simphiwe in a public imagination, it is not one that is highly circulated in the conventional senses of how public spheres work. Although there is a shared sense of what Simphiwe can imaginatively stand for – what Malik characterised as Afropolitan femininity – the manner in which the idea of her is used here is still quite curious.

As you read this chapter, maybe you have your own ideas about what is going on here. You may have decided that this is a type of man and then proceeded to judge what that means about such a man's interior and external life. I am less interested in what kind of man this is, than in making sense of what has just happened here in the story I am telling. I am immediately struck by several things.

First, this narrative and dance are not really about Simphiwe Dana at all. It does not really matter to me whether by some coincidence both men had brief flings with her. She is an adult woman and therefore entitled to a life of her choosing with men who clearly place a lot of effort into pursuing a certain 'type' of woman. I can see what the attraction would be until they start trying so hard to act evolved.

Second, Zuko and Donald are making very clear assumptions about me, even though, again, much of this does not pertain to me as an individual in the world at all. There is some typification or classification of me and Simphiwe as shorthand for something else. This something else is really about a certain relationship of masking masculinity. Conservative masculinities will use anything at their disposal to get their end result. Here, it seemed that the end result could only be attained through feigning a vulnerable masculinity.

Third, Simphiwe Dana is evoked here to symbolise something about masculinity. More specifically, it is about the pretence at a certain desirable masculinity. Zuko and Donald are guessing that if they show themselves to be the kind of men that Simphiwe desires, it will then follow that another *type* of woman, assumed to include me, will also find them worthy of a second glance, and a chance of dalliance.

What I actually read their masculinity as performing is laziness. They do not want to work and take a chance at performing a type of masculinity that they imagine I might find desirable. But they nonetheless want the credit that they imagine accrues to the kind of men who actually make an effort. Even if they really did have brief associations with Simphiwe, they are still being lazy in relying on shorthand. This is partly annoying and partly insulting to the women concerned, even though there is also a grain of truth to what they are saying and performing about how women make men desirable to each other. I told an extremely promiscuous man once that the reason women still want to sleep with him is because of the collective aura of the 'cool women' who have slept with him (mostly secretly because they have self-preservation) in the past. He still carried some of their energy. I know this is not scientific, but I was only *half* joking when I told him this.

Let us turn to the truth factor in the Zuko/Donald scenario. It is not whether or not they have been with Simphiwe. It is what women read into the actions of other women within the realm of heterosexual pleasure and romance. Women do take other women's opinions very seriously in the area of sexuality, in good and bad ways. We all have some memory of an uninteresting man getting the excited attention of a fascinating woman. Her interest very often made us wonder about him. In a good sense, we might start to think that this man cannot be *that* boring if *she* is interested. When we were in our teen years and twenties, my friend and cousin, Thoko Barnabas, used to like saying that when a woman shows obvious interest in being with a man that other women have written off, she makes other women wonder about her man's hidden characteristics. Most women will do nothing but feed this fascination. Some, however, will then try to find out what is so interesting about this man, often in quite abrasive ways for the woman concerned. Patriarchy, after all, makes women very competitive and it also says that no matter how amazing a woman is, the ultimate reward is being chosen (back) by a heterosexual man – or an assumed heterosexual man. Although Thoko was the first person to articulate this to me, I have recognised this as played out in much popular cultural material, be it women's magazines or romantic comedies.

My two suitors are relying on this knowledge that women watch other women's choices for sex, romance and coupling. They are both being lazy and not really making an effort to *be* interesting, engage me or really charm me. They do not worry that Simphiwe's privacy is a battering tool, a commodity in the patriarchal trade of desirability. Instead of acting in ways that render them desirable, they are telling me that Simphiwe desires or once desired them and therefore I should too.

As an adult, I understand that when you want to be with someone sexually and/or romantically, there is a mating dance required. All flirtation is a sort of play. We all use a range of resources available to us. We want returned desire, not rejection. I also understand that much of this flirtation requires stepping into certain roles, and that all of these roles require some economic use of the truth. So, whether you are the kind of person who takes on whatever personality the object of your affection likes in order to get his/her/their attention or whether you simply get your hair done or wax just before you go on a date, put on your favourite perfume or jewellery just before seeing that person, you are participating in this dance. I also understand that every incarnation of the mating dance carries the risk of rejection.

Zuko's and Donald's individual and collective dances with me are about maximising the chances of being desired back. They are drawn to a certain kind of woman, of the sort of Simphiwe, whom they assume is the kind of woman I will also find attractive. I do find her attractive. She is a genius, very smart in real life, well read, fun, brave, takes chances and risks both privately and publicly, gives very generously of herself and demands what she requires without making apologies for it. But finding a woman attractive and fascinating is not going to automatically translate into being

41

attracted to the same profile of men that she is apparently drawn to. They can also see some of the things I value without having to be too close to me: intellectual life, fairness, creativity.

But there are also other things going on here.

Zuko and Donald are completely missing the point. Simphiwe and I do have shared traits in people that we are drawn to. A mere glimpse at friends we have in common will show some of the people we like to be with, and find joy in being around. Some of the characteristics are: politically minded people who speak sometimes quite forcefully about what they believe even if it is not fashionable, people who are not afraid to think critically even when this is risky, people who are worldly and citizens of more than one tribe, people who value the arts in one way or another, whether or not they themselves produce art, people who read widely as part of work and pleasure, people who are sometimes incredibly intense but also fun. Laughter is a huge part of both of our lives individually. We are drawn to people who are not threatened by difference and who embrace a certain politics on sexual orientation, and people who are not committed to rigid gender roles. But we also have very significant differences and inflect even those shared preferred tastes quite differently. I am not a soft feminist at all. Simphiwe describes herself in this manner, although I think her feminism has been growing some edge in the last few months, contradictions notwithstanding. Simphiwe also has a higher tolerance for personality types I cannot really bear to be around, and more fluctuation in her friendship circles than I do. Most of my friendships date from childhood, school and university in the early 1990s, although I have a handful of strong friendships from the last decade.

Did I believe Zuko and Donald? Yes and no.

I believed that there had been some flirtation with one. I thought one was lying. It did not matter greatly to me where truth resided in their stories because neither one was in the running for a meaningful relationship with me even before the declarations that are the subject of this chapter. This is partly because of their own biographies, irrespective of what they had just told me about themselves, but also because of what it is that I was prepared to consider for myself at that time.

Because I do not want to give the impression that they are the same person, it may be useful to say something about how 'different' these very similar men are. Zuko is in a complicated polyamorous arrangement with three formally recognised women partners, and I suspect also with a man that he both works with and spends much time speaking amorously about. He self-identifies as heterosexual and spends some time making this 'clear' in how closely he watches men he reads as gay even though he would not ordinarily associate himself with homophobic sentiments.

Donald had recently exited a relationship, is considerably younger but will not reveal his exact age, and is known to prefer women older than he is.

They both have very carefully cultivated 'public' personalities that are often out of step with how they really live.

If we assume for a minute that they are inappropriately revealing events that did, in fact, happen, rather than fantasy, we still have to reckon with the fact that Simphiwe did not have public relationships with them or even revealed relations with them in this way. Both of them choose to make her private life public, and their manner of proceeding left me in no doubt that they had shared this information with other women before. Each one of these men, in different ways, assumes that he is entitled to Simphiwe as a resource in very different ways. Indirectly, they are saying that, after the end of the claimed romantic association, she matters to the extent that she is useful to make them attractive but her boundaries and privacy were not important enough to protect from me, someone they were only getting to know. It is very odd that they want to convince me that they are decent and sophisticated men by showing disregard for another woman, who is also my friend, at the end of their intimacy with her.

One Saturday afternoon, as I discussed the outline for the remaining parts of the book as part of negotiating different deadlines with my publisher, I told Melinda the story of the two men, briefly, while my friend, Naledi, sat at my kitchen table with us. A few days after this exchange, Naledi guessed Zuko's identity. Without waiting for me to confirm or rebut who she had named, she then told me specific details he had revealed to her. I had previously only mentioned the claim, not the specific narratives of what Zuko claimed has happened where. Yet what she shared matched what Zuko had shared with me.

I am not interested in the morality of this exchange or behaviour. I am, however, intrigued by what is happening when men with some degree of success, who are neither unattractive nor undesired by precisely the kind of woman they profess to be attracted to, choose these particular ways to speak about themselves.

What was it that made them think it was attractive to put an iconic woman's life on display in this manner as part of their mating dance with other women? Adult women have casual encounters all the time, whether we speak about them or not, even in a society where the tenor of sexual conversation is so conservative. What kind of masculinity legitimises itself through the disrespect of such private encounters at the same time that it participates in them?

It is an attempt to legitimise themselves at her expense. It should be unsurprising in a society such as ours, where women's lives, women's loves and sexual expression are all very differently regulated.

The paradox for me is that two, seemingly mutually exclusive processes seem to be at work here: Simphiwe is both being placed on a pedestal (if she had flirtations with them, then other women most likely will want to) and subjected to the most bizarre attempt at domestication (she is not that special. She can be belittled, rendered just a sexual body, like *any other* woman). This may be a paradox, but within patriarchal regulation of femininity and masculinity, paradoxes are not unusual. Think about chivalry and intimate partner violence, or the virgin-mother and whore dynamic.

In his seminal study, *Ways of Seeing,* John Berger shows how over several centuries, women's bodies and presences have not only been used to signal a certain masculine virility, but that this relied on the women being reduced to the level of accessory to the man concerned. Ironically, this ability to signal that certain women could be accessories rested on the male lover's capacity to demonstrate ownership of the woman's body. Successful demonstration of this 'ownership' of the woman took on value once paraded in public, for example, in nude paintings in the public sections of the homes of wealthy men in Europe and, later, in galleries. The woman in the painting signalled a certain wealth for the man. If he was commissioning paintings of her and landscapes of his property, he could afford the commission. Ownership and display of the artwork signalled this to his visitors and those he entertained in his home. He owned both the painting and what was within its frame: the land/woman. A contemporary manifestation of this exists in many music videos in kwaito, rap, pop, rock and other genres where women's bodies say something about a man having arrived – the more women, called and rendered as 'video ho's' or 'video vixens', he has demonstrated access to. This use of women's bodies is also in line with the distinction that Berger draws between the nude and being naked:

> To be naked is to be oneself. To be nude is to be seen naked
> by others and yet not recognized for oneself. A naked body
> has to be seen as an object in order to become a nude.

But fully dressed women's bodily presence often functions in exactly the same kinds of ways across music genres. They are not there *as* themselves, but to signal something made visible about the male singer/rapper/band members who perform the musical product being executed.

While Simphiwe's body was not in a painting in the estates of these men, Zuko's and Donald's retelling of trysts with her was designed to elevate them and render her as the embodied accessory. While the women that Berger writes about did not need to be famous, and indeed some of their names have disappeared from history once their authorising gesture is achieved, there are nonetheless linkages with what is at play here.

It is clear that although these men may well like to boast about their virility and conquests, something about what Simphiwe signifies works better than the use of lesser known and less accomplished women. Simphiwe, here, works contradictorily: as bait or object that is not important in/of itself, as well as prime jewel in Zuko's and Donald's crowns. She needs to be a body on display in order for them to perform desirable masculinity.

Reducing a woman who occupies the public sphere for her brain, courage and/or talent to her vagina is an established way of trivialising women in South Africa. One of the better known photographic images of 1in9 activists in purple T-shirts protesting outside court shows several placards with the words 'not just faces and vaginas'. Like all of 1in9's direct actions, this statement challenges highly circulated hetero-patriarchal assumptions about women's place in South Africa. For Simphiwe Dana, a more public enactment of this was the revelation of her affair with a kwaito group member turned pastor. One Sunday morning in February 2012, South Africa woke up to news that Simphiwe had been carrying on an affair with a married man. The man had once been in a music group made of two sets of twins. South Africa's memory of this man's and his group's name was so vague that the same old pictures of the group from the 1990s were recycled over and over again as visual memory aid. What was striking in all the coverage was the manner in which Simphiwe Dana was slut-shamed: she was marked as the immoral woman who was having sex with a married man at the same time that she had constantly tweeted on the virtues of heterosexual monogamy as it culminates in marriage. (I return to Simphiwe's stance on marriages of different kinds in part 2 of Desiring Simphiwe). The attacks on Twitter were so virulent that she withdrew to lick her wounds, and at the time of writing this, many months later, she has not returned to even half of her previous social media presence. The attacks were not just attempts to hold her accountable for the inconsistency between her social media declarations, on the one hand, and her recent affair, on the other. She was slut-shamed, which is a phenomenon in which women are policed, taunted and censored for participating in sexual behaviour which transgresses conventional patriarchal sexual conduct. Slut-shaming is performed publicly against a woman, and marks her as sexually out of control and inappropriate and seeks to induce guilt. Such slut-shaming is also evident in the popular Twitter trend of ridiculing 'side-chicks'. Women thus named are not the 'official' girlfriend/partner/wife of any man, but have a secondary relationship with him. There is rarely any mention of the offending man who strays from the official relationship, just like there is no male equivalent for a 'side-chick'.

This outcry provoked by a woman who had acted against the sacred union of marriage would have been understandable were it not for the numerous inconsistencies that are rife in the area of sexuality in South Africa. Whereas Simphiwe was held accountable for her double-speak on fidelity, as she should have been, the former kwaito group member and married man was able to escape much of the public censure. This is because he is a man, and South Africa is very quick to forgive men who veer off from the monogamous fidelity path.

Secondly, while she initially tried to shield him from the embarrassment, admitting that she loved him but would not name him, as cited in various newspapers, including *City Press* on 26 February 2012 and thereafter, he chose to save himself once discovered. In various papers, he was cited as claiming that his association with her had been a brief indiscretion, that he later felt sorry for her and that he loved his wife.

He was not and could not be slut-shamed because male virility grows through association with multiple partners, whereas women's standing is constantly in danger of tarnish because of who they may or may not have had sex with. Even when it is the man who is married and the woman not, the woman bears the sole brunt of the indiscretion. We very often forgive and later reward men who act in defiance of the same vows they professed. That *this man* is a hypocrite too seemed minor even though he was also a man of the cloth, and had therefore transgressed two institutional commitments to his wife and their marriage, on the one hand, as well as to the Church where heterosexual marriage is a central foundation, on the other.

Because of the society we live in, however, where women's desire is perpetually pathologised and regulated unless it is expressed within heterosexual marriage, the repetition of these claims to Simphiwe's body also work against her. While these men speak about themselves through Simphiwe, they do so in a manner that speaks against her. To become better men, they need to publicly shame and betray her. There are various ways to achieve 'better man' status. They can do so like Zuko and Donald, through the rendering public of something that should be private between two available and consenting adults. Or, they can recast her as a sexual being in semi-public spaces, focusing attention away from why she is in the spotlight in the first place.

One of the ways in which women's work is routinely trivialised in South African society, and elsewhere, is through the mention of the women's sexual expression or sexual partners. We see this in the asymmetrical reference to women in the public domain – who achieve visibility through their own work as activists, intellectuals, artists – through being appended to famous men. So, for example, Winnie Madikizela Mandela is constantly referred to as Nelson Mandela's former wife, as though the whole world does not know exactly who Ms Madikizela Mandela is through her own work. The obituaries after Albertina Sisulu's death expressed this same sentiment. It continues to happen to Dr Mamphela Ramphele, whose remarkable life has seen her achieve stunning success across six radically different terrains in her young life: Black Consciousness activism that saw her establish several clinics that are still running as I write this, a medical career followed by a productive academic research life after getting her PhD in Anthropology, a vice chancellorship at the University of Cape Town, authoring the first sexual harassment in the workplace policy in South Africa which quickly became the blueprint for workplaces nationally, success in business while maintaining an active writing and public intellectual life. But she continues to be haunted by the slur of being Steve Biko's mistress, and in a relentless form of slut-shaming is often discussed primarily in these terms to trivialise or ignore whatever intellectual point she makes. It does not matter that they were comrades, that he was her 'mistress' too, or that as phenomenal a legacy as he left us, he has been dead for almost four decades, while she has continued to make remarkable impact on the world. For those hell-bent on silencing her, she becomes the perpetual 'side-chick'.

I could refer to many other examples. Phyllis Ntantala's writing shows how this is not a recent phenomenon, but that it nonetheless continues to be effective in making women who are out of control and powerful in their own right much smaller. I spent considerable time on this phenomenon in my published academic work on Black women's intellectual legacies in South Africa, in *Becoming Worthy Ancestors: Archive, public deliberation and identity in South Africa*, a collection edited by Xolela Mangcu. The domestication of Simphiwe may not work successfully for Zuko and Donald sometimes because they chose the wrong audiences, audiences made up of women like Naledi and me, who find these kinds of masculine performances off-putting rather than attractive.

CHAPTER 4

Desiring Simphiwe 2:
The soft feminist

*Only by learning to live in harmony with your
contradictions can you keep it all afloat.*

Audre Lorde

*Be nobody's darling
Be an outcast
Take the contradictions
Of your life
And wrap around
You like a shawl,
To parry stones
To keep you warm*

Alice Walker

*I call it soul music, not because it falls within a
certain genre, but because it is music you can feel.*

Simphiwe Dana

As a woman, no matter how successful you look, even a beggar on the street believes they own your body. I have experienced this. "Hello nice, hello baby!" Some men will even go the length of touching you, grabbing you. You have to put on a bulletproof mask when you leave your house, so that you may not be emotionally incensed enough to want to lash out in anger.

Instead of changing the vampiric nature of patriarchal society, we try to change the victim. Maybe you must dress differently, maybe change your attitude, we say.

Patriarchy is a power game. Woe unto you if you step in the path of a powerless, patriarchal male. He will make you pay for the pain of his emasculation. He does not even have to know you to punish you for his disappointments.

Simphiwe Dana 'Corrective rape and
our naked reality'

Story 1

A group of us are sitting around on a warm Johannesburg Sunday afternoon eating, drinking, chatting loudly and generally having a good time. Our children are making a mess of epic proportions and mostly not in the kitchen, where we have all ended up. We are discussing politics, parenting, sexuality and a certain African American writer. We disagree on a range of things. There are several parents, people who have decided never to parent, and a few undecided ones. We are a mix of genders, sexual orientations, languages and nationalities. All of us are Black. We are all hopeless romantics and cynics at the same time, but different cocktail combinations of these two are in each one of us. I am talking about finally doing something about my huge desire for another child and different suggestions are flying about the room. None of my friends are really paying attention to what I have already decided to do. Instead, they continue to discuss 'my options'. One of the women suggests that I might fall in love. The rest of us pretend not to see the connection between that and the topic. She humours us, and getting dreamier and dreamier-eyed, insists that when I fall in love next time, a child will seal the deal. She is not the only one getting dreamy-eyed. We all think this is hilarious. Surely, none of us *really* believe in children sealing romantic deals.

Story 2

When Simphiwe talks to Thando Pato about motherhood and work, her own parenting story and feelings are intertwined with her memory of being mothered as a little girl by a mother who also had a working life. First, her own narrative:

> The last time I went on tour, I was gone first for four weeks and then the second time for two weeks. When I left the first time, I thought I was going to go on holiday. Being a mother is fun but you need a break. The first week was fine, but by the end of the tour I had to call home at least every four hours. I felt so bad because my kids were thousands of kilometres away. Being a mother feels like one of my biggest weaknesses because I can't be there all the time. But I guess all mothers feel that way.

Then a memory of a mother's love, recognising anxiety in retrospect:

> I remember the first time we went to stay with uMama. She was a nurse by then and when she saw us she just broke down and cried, right there. And for the next month, it was torture for us because she was scrubbing us and feeding us raw eggs and all sorts of healthy things... I guess we were in a terrible state and we just didn't realise it, but we hated breakfast lunch and supper. We just loved meat and bread. But when I think about it she was trying to make up for lost time because she felt bad. But there was no reason for it because she did her best.

In all patriarchal societies, motherhood, mothers and mothering are loaded with unwieldy burdens. A former friend of mine was pained before she remarked on how awful the mothering literature is for pregnant women, already called 'expectant mothers'. She noted, reading my books and magazines which I obsessively pored over during my own pregnancy, that the material was in different turns loaded with guilt and fear. I have since had this conversation with other feminist mothers who seek to manage the constant haunting of inadequacy. Thus, while motherhood is romanticised as easy, instinctual and as that which completes women, it is often fraught terrain.

As a child, both my parents were professionals: my mother a nursing sister and my father a lecturer in Organic Chemistry. Everybody I knew had parents that worked. It never occurred to me that there was anything wrong with women who worked outside the home. I assumed it was normal and everywhere. Yet, as the parent of a small child, I am constantly struck by the scheduling of many school activities – and listen to many professional working women bemoan the same – which assumes that the mother will have time in the middle of the day for all manner of time-consuming activities from volunteering for Wednesday morning library duty to cooking at noon for some school fundraiser. Working women of all classes negotiate the anxiety of not being there all the time that Simphiwe talks about. We are all fed the ideology that says that we should prioritise *mothering* above all else. This is part of what Simphiwe is pointing to, in both her own and her mother's anxiety. We all love our children and want the best for them. But many of us also choose to be ourselves.

Story 3
As a little girl growing into a young woman, she is told constantly that if she has a baby, she will have to get a job and support it. If you are old enough to make it, you are old enough to take care of it. Keep your legs closed, she is told. Do not be like those other girls. Her parents watch her like a hawk but pretend not to. She knows she can speak her mind, knows the boundaries of

precociousness and disrespect, and does not have a child while still at school. She is a good girl, which is not the same thing as a virgin. She walks several thin lines at once. For girls in her class, there is a very thin line between not being 'like those loose girls' and being unable to protect yourself at 12 from a teacher whose previous students did not finish school and now sell vegetables in town because they fell pregnant. Another thin line exists between having sort of consensual sex in her teens and pretending to be a virgin to her parents. It is there again between resenting her parents' over-protectiveness and wishing they trusted her more. When she is 25, an aunt asks her about the missing cows for her, wonders aloud about why she does not *even* have a child to show for all her years. Without changing her behaviour, she has moved from a good girl to a spinster, even though nobody says that word anymore. Nobody wants to marry a know-it-all-show-off. Her father insists that she needs to finish all the degrees she wants before getting married. Love always returns, he says. Finish what you want first. When she gets her PhD, his pride is obvious. Later, he says 'now you can live your life, *sisi*. Just do what makes you happy.'

Audre Lorde's and Alice Walker's quotations at the top of this chapter both take an attitude to contradictions that says we should own and embrace our personal ones, rather than try to resolve them. Simphiwe's approach seems to resemble theirs, even though I have never heard her say so. She may even disagree with me on this. Lorde says whatever we do with our contradictions, they should stop being bothersome because otherwise we cannot survive. Walker suggests that we should use our contradictions like a shield to ward off the criticisms and attacks that we will get for refusing to be self-censoring.

We all live with an untidy mess of contradictions. It is the human condition. We may not always pay attention to them or call them such, but if we lived with relentless consistency and tidiness, we would cease to function. 'Identity is never complete', as the Jamaican/British genius who changed how the global academy thinks about culture, identity and how media works, Stuart Hall, insists. Hall's expansive work teaches us that identity is an endless process, that as human beings individually and collectively, we are in constant formation and re-formation. And our contradictions are part of this process. However, there is a point at which contradictions become hypocrisy, so I am not making an argument for hypocrisy. This 'point' is a difficult one to identify because it is also one of unmanageability and credibility. The point of hypocrisy has been reached when we are living a lie. But even stating it in this way is not as straight forward as it seems.

When you are a woman in South Africa today, staying alive requires constantly keeping your eye on that point in order to juggle your contradictions whilst staying away from hypocrisy. Yes, there *are* women who are hypocrites. But I am talking about the majority who are not.

This chapter is subtitled 'the soft feminist' for several reasons. The first and most important motivation is due to the fact that this is what Simphiwe calls herself sometimes. I asked her what she meant by this at the tail end of one of our disagreements. I no longer remember whether it was about monogamy and marriage or something else. She told me that describing herself as a soft feminist meant that *although* she was blatantly opposed to patriarchy, she still desired a strong man. I am not sure what she meant by a strong man that required what I have used 'although' to signal here.

The second reason I use the appellation for her is because I agree that Simphiwe regularly articulates a feminist stance, that many of her career and personal choices surface a feminist consciousness. All feminists are a *kind* of feminist, even though sometimes misogynists like to pretend we are aliens who think with one centrally controlled brain, like The Uni-mind in *Toy Story* 2000 spin off film *Buzz Light Year of Star Command*. So, by 'a kind of feminist', I clearly recognise feminist motivation and embattlement in much that she does, chooses, rejects and strives for both personally and politically. To say we may not be the same *kind* of feminist simply means the layers of our feminism are not identical.

I think Simphiwe's feminist consciousness comes across very clearly in three aspects of her public (and private) life: her self-representation in relation to her music, her romantic choices, her stance on commitment and what she unsettles through these. It is equally evident in her refusal to be submissive to any text, not even the ostensibly questioning ones.

The Ugandan law professor and feminist, Sylvia Tamale argues that there is immense pressure on women to adhere to domesticity. Tamale's explication of what domesticity entails is very important for me because, like many people, I am otherwise wont to think of domesticity less adventurously. I want to insert what she says about domesticity here in its entirety:

> Domesticity as an ideology is historically and culturally constructed and is closely linked to patriarchy, gender/power relations and the artificial private/public distinction. The way patriarchy defines women is such that their full and wholesome existence depends on getting married, producing children and caring for her family. In Africa, it does not matter whether a woman is a successful politician, possesses three PhDs and runs the most successful business in town; if she has never married and/or is childless, she is perceived to be lacking in a fundamental way. Girl children are raised and socialised into this ideology and few ever question or challenge its basic tenets. Single, childless women carry a permanent stigma like a lodestone about their necks. They are viewed by society as halfbaked, even half-human. Thus, the domestic roles of mother, wife and homemaker become the key constructions of women's identity in Africa.

For Tamale, very importantly, it is not that women are kept in domestic spheres, and, consequently, away from the influential public sphere that matters, because this is a false division. Rather, it is that what happens in the domestic area of the home, marriage, reproduction and sexuality is the most important part of women's recognition as human in patriarchal societies. In other words, whatever women do with their lives, they are most valuable when they have ticked the boxes in terms of adhering to the expectations of domesticity as Tamale defines it. I will illustrate how this expectation of 'ticking the boxes' of domesticity appears in relation to how professional women are valued and devalued in public South African life.

Simphiwe is not particularly respectful of the limitations posed by the ideology of domesticity. Although there are many scripts for femininity that are available to Simphiwe, and are highly subscribed to by those in the music and entertainment industries, her choices on aesthetics and self-representation often show a much more eccentric and imaginative range of femininities than those available in domesticity. Her radically different choices are clear both in her videos and beyond. To begin to illustrate some of these expressions of her 'soft-feminism', let me first turn to render visible what I see as the most dominant trope of economically mobile and successful femininity in post-apartheid public culture. Although she is South African, famous, beautiful, talented and mobile, Simphiwe very clearly does not subscribe to this trope that I call 'the new South African woman'. The new South African woman also clearly illustrates something about Tamale's domesticity ideology, because, while domesticity is universal, it does not find the exact same expression everywhere in the world. Instead, it is coloured by different contexts even though it retains the same core.

But who is the new South African woman?

The 'new South African woman' is a working woman. She has a career, is ambitious and driven. She has smooth skin, straight, shiny hair and tastefully manicured nails. This means that she either has light coloured acrylic tips or pastel coloured nails. Occasionally she has a stronger colour on her nails, but never one that shows too much character, so deep reds and all greys are allowed but yellow has excessive personality. Her brow is shaped by waxing, threading or tweezing so that the end of her brow is aligned to the outer eye corner. She has hairless armpits and knows where to get a Brazilian, a Bollywood or a Hollywood wax but she does not talk about it. She speaks neither too loudly nor too softly, and fluently in English. She looks like the women who read the news on SABC3 bulletins, but does not necessarily read as widely or live like them.

She aspires to have an address in the suburbs and will rent at the desired address rather than buy in a less prestigious area where she can afford to buy property. She says 'corporate' when she speaks about work, and uses the phrase 'work life balance' when speaking of living a full life. The new South African woman is a skilled consumer. She reads several women's magazines, some newspapers, is knowledgeable and has an opinion but frowns on women who are forceful with their ideas. She is assumed to be heterosexual, aspires to marriage in her late twenties, two cars in her household and travel outside the continent. She goes to a designer or prosperity church. If she is already married, she knows that prayer, not letting herself go and keeping things spicy is the way to a lasting marriage, but she is not morally opposed to divorce under the right circumstances. She knows how to take care of her man, knows that you should never tell a man everything about your money and birth family, and she reads Steve Harvey *just in case*.

This woman does not just believe in women's empowerment; she lives it. She is not a feminist because she rather believes in feminine power and does not think women should act like men. She is happy when more women join the workforce but worries about the possibility of having a woman boss. When she speaks of a PhD, she is not referring to a doctorate but the hyped 'pull her down' syndrome. She does not like the idea of sharing her man, but recognises that men are likely to stray; but she is either monogamous or pretends to be. She has a vision board as well as a favourite motivational speaker or writer. She is the consummate professional, punctual and committed to personal development. She has a five-year plan and a ten-year plan and does not compromise on her 'me-time'. She may drink or smoke moderately. If she does so excessively, she does so in private because discretion is everything.

There is absolutely nothing wrong with being this woman. She does represent some women very well.

Although most women in South Africa do not fit this profile, this woman gets the most airplay. Part of what it does to watch the same image over and over again, is that it becomes naturalised and invisible. We stop seeing her and start to take her as a given, as representative, as the idea of femininity to which women should aspire. She becomes normal. Whenever we construct normal, we also construct abnormal.

Women characters transform into her time and again in *Generations*, *Isidingo* and other national soapies and dramas. We read about her in the women's magazines we love and see her interviewed, often asked the same questions that start with flagging her status as a 'professional, wife and mother' and 'juggling these'. She may come in as a 'rural girl', 'township girl' or start out as a model, but she soon transforms into the new South African woman and entrepreneur. She may even think of her image as governed more by 'brand' than reputation.

There are several disturbing factors to her. I have already alluded to the first, where she becomes the aspirational archetype: the woman we should all transform into if our dreams come true. Getting as close to her as possible is how we start to matter and to show that we have really 'made it'. If we can afford the designer wear and German cars that accompany this success, all the better.

Second, creating such a mould obscures the fact that women come in all sorts of formats, as does women's desire. This erases the real diversity that women live, dream about, feel and create deliberately every day.

Third, most women cannot afford this life and therefore need to go into debt in order to approximate her. When they do, we blame them for being conspicuous consumers or 'gold-diggers'.

Finally, when the new South African woman finishes reconstructing herself, she needs to publicly stick to the formula. Otherwise, we begin to see her set foot on another course, one that is less fairy-tale and more tragic heroine, also known as the train wreck. Because she is always in danger of being exposed as a fraud, she has to constantly show her prowess across all three sectors in her life in order to remain a good 'wife, mother, professional'.

The public appetite for her is also the same one for women as train wrecks, so in order to stay in the desirable category, she has to constantly demonstrate that she successfully juggles. She has access to public mobility upwards but she is inevitably haunted by the suggestion that she might be a bit of a disaster or accident-prone if prompted and asked about her private life.

In real life these women who break moulds have to demonstrate that they are 'conventional women' in private in order to escape the same kind of censor, and in order to retain recognition as the women we emulate. Some women have clearly mastered the formula and are able to stay on top of the public adoration game for great lengths of time. Whether actual women really live in this way is beside the point. Those who stay adherent to New South African Woman status constantly have to tick certain kinds of boxes, otherwise they become train wrecks regardless of their public successes.

Professional women are always advised that overachiever women are threatening to men, and that therefore, women should go out of their way to be desirable to men. This is code for not 'letting yourself go', further assisted by the constant mention of the shortage of men in South Africa, which is really just a ruse to terrorise women into staying manageable. The fact that the gender ratio is skewed in favour of men, aggravated by the growing popularity of polygamy again from the terrain of the unofficial to actual increased visibility, is part of the promise of the family that every woman must achieve if she is to be a 'success'.

If she occasionally shares information about a tragedy or hardship in her life, she feeds the train wreck appetite and buys herself more public air time. This is the real price for women 'having it all': the constant reminder in patriarchal society that they cannot, in fact, have it all. They need to feed the monster with parts of themselves that can metaphorically grow back if the monster is not to consume them wholesale.

The celebrated family script is always the heterosexual one, usually with a husband and wife, ultimately, where everybody is heterosexual. Family is also seen as the 'natural' kind with bonds of blood, not the constructed kind. The family is not just heterosexual, though. It also comes with a whole range of other assumptions. As visual scholar Patricia Zimmerman reminds us, family often assumes the presence of a 'strong father, supportive mother, and dutiful children'. This idea is then also projected onto other sites in the society, and therefore works in both naturalising and as 'central organizing principle'. Try thinking about the last five times you read articles in the South African mainstream press, or watched characters on South African television, that reflected a radically different mode of femininity and family life. Try thinking about how many times such characters and families are sympathetically rendered. We are constantly bombarded with a very narrow framework for femininity and family life.

Yet, this is obviously a con because most women are doing it alone. That is what the statistics say. The South African Institute of Race Relations research shows that the norm in contemporary South Africa is a family where the only present parent is the mother, and that in 2010 only 35% of children live with two parents. These two-parent households are not all heterosexual. The script is not working and women are placed in a position where they have to constantly re-write it. There are endless complications that come with rewriting it. And all the complications are flirtations with that point of hypocrisy: aspiring to be the new South African Woman, but deviating from the script when no one is looking.

Real women have all sorts of desires. Sometimes we like multiple piercings and lip gloss, sex with men and women separately. Sometimes real women do not believe in God and have no desire for straight hair or sanitized dreadlocks. Real women often want casual sex for its own sake without having to be judged as immoral or out of control.

Simphiwe Dana's life is also a staging of some of these complications, for, while she deliberately flouts many of the conventions associated with the archetype I have outlined above, she also, at the same time, battles with the romantic narrative that comes with patriarchal femininity, regulated in our time through the new South African woman. From the time we can talk, we are taught incessantly about appropriate ways of being girls and women, and the vast majority of these are patriarchal. The ways in which we often think about romance is also deeply patriarchal. I described the men and women around my kitchen table as both romantic and cynical. Although all of us self-identify as feminist, the manner in which we negotiate the contradictions that come with our desire for certain kinds of femininity and masculinity differ. That half-joke that one of my friends makes is humorous because to varying degrees we all *do* desire aspects of the romance narrative that is dominant in our society at the same time that we recognise the many lies in its promise of contentment.

Simphiwe's self-representation, her styling and her lifestyle are clearly not in pursuit of the new South African woman ideal. She deliberately distances herself from it, not through judgment of those who choose it, but through embracing different alternatives. Her own sense of aesthetics is evident from her personal and professional style. Many of these choices are evident in her public self-representation, in what she says about herself, which aspects of her life she allows into the public glare, in as much as they are evident in many aesthetic choices that frame her career.

Having chosen her as the cover girl for their August 2010 issue, the London-based *New African Woman*, a lifestyle magazine 'for the discerning woman' characterised her as 'The goddess of African cool'. Inside the magazine, the article's author, Masanda Peter begins by recalling all the comparisons that have peppered Simphiwe's career, calling her variously 'the African Erykah Badu, Lauryn Hill, Corinne Bailey Rae, and even Norah Jones' before finally deciding that the most apt and flattering accolade is of her as 'the best thing to happen to African soul jazz since Miriam Makeba'.

The fact that Peter chooses these particular artists before deciding on Makeba, and that it is a list rather than a 'type' can be read in a variety of ways. These musicians are not the same kind of artist except to the extent that they are all a) very distinctive in their artistry and therefore difficult to categorise in terms of genre, and b) very unafraid of their voices. Masanda Peter is doing more than simply relating Simphiwe Dana's musical persona to other artists with a world presence. There is something to these particular linkages Peter makes, beyond the South African obsession with all validations 'international' and 'world class'. It seems Peter is developing a language to speak about aspects of Ms Dana's musical persona in ways that show her as both exceptional and headstrong, and showing that she makes sense in her choices.

In a Malaysian interview in February 2012, Erykah Badu said her personal aesthetic style is 'dancerish' because she likes to move and feel 'deconstructed not perfect'. Because this interview happened just before a concert in Kuala Lumpur, which was later cancelled by the Malaysian government, Daphne Iking asks Ms Badu what the audience can expect. This is the latter's answer:

> I hope you don't expect anything. I hope people don't expect anything. I hope people come preparing themselves to eliminate things because we don't mind if you live it with us. That's what it's for. I can tell you what I plan to do. I plan to just come have church and therapy. And I hope that people feel good. Or bad. Or something. Just feel.

Perhaps she is being difficult. However, we can also read Erykah Badu to be saying that the most important thing she hopes for in the concert is a communion between musicians on stage and those who had paid to attend. Both the 'dancerish' aesthetic and the stress on feeling something tell us something about the performance. But what they tell us is abstract. She is saying: expect to be part of the same spiritual, healing experience that the performers will also be part of. Church and therapy are about interiority. Interestingly, the musician is saying it is not just the look and sound that matter, but also how they make you feel. She is saying that the music is *also* in the feelings of all involved.

This sentiment is not radically different from one expressed by Lauryn Hill after her 2010 Rock the Bells New York performance, where she discussed coming back after several years of withdrawal from public performances and appearances. In a *Hiphop Shop* interview (from the Fuse channel), following her own performance, she told Tourè that she had been away from the spotlight because she wanted normalcy for herself and her children, and had now returned because:

> I think I am ready to express myself again. You have to live life so you have something substantial to share, or it's kinda pointless and vain. I don't think I ever did music just for attention or to be seen, you know. I really did it because it also stimulated me. I was excited about the challenge and challenges of making music... I think I am a pioneer spirit and when you can't do that because you feel a certain claustrophobia, it was counter-productive, so I needed to make my own space again.

Ms Hill is saying that she needs to feel like she has something worthy to share with audiences in order to be public, rather than simply engaging in a vain, attention-grabbing or attention-hogging exercise. But she is saying much more than this because the vanity she does not embrace musically also takes something away from her. It makes it hard for her to breathe. It suffocates her. Therefore when she has nothing to say publicly, there is no point in making public music. What feeds her creativity, and excites her about making music, is the ability to do something new, to occupy this place of a 'pioneer spirit'.

What Hill is saying here is in tune with what Badu says before her in the chronology of this chapter: making music is an expression of sacred bonding between artist and listeners. It is not simply a show or entertainment. This is something similar to what Corrine Bailey Rae also speaks about in a VUZU TV interview, with an unidentified interviewer, by declaring that one of the best things about being a musician is the fact that musicians' curiosity offers 'a passport into places, so I feel that all this stuff is open to me' The 'stuff' she speaks about is the whole world (of experiences and feelings) as well as the 'stuff' of other creative people's processes. In other words, musical identity and the making of music gives her access to a range of realities and possibilities.

Finally, Norah Jones tells Brad Wete in the June/July 2012 issue of the Canadian music magazine, *Complex:*

> I'd rather have critical acclaim than pop glory. It would make me crazy to obsess about where I stand with people. I walk a fine line between having a lot of success and selling out – and I'm not a pop star. I'm not out there like that. I just love music. If I wanted to be on the Hot 100, I would have chosen a different musical path. I'd rather cook than be served. I like to have more control, but I'm not as bad as Meg Ryan in *When Harry Met Sally*. I've found the balance between cooking and not overdoing it. I like to cook simple things and not spend hours stressing over meals.

If we listen to Jones, here, again, is the insistence that what she does is neither for approval nor for fame, at a time where entire lives are changed for the chance at fame. As scholars of celebrity culture tell us, we live in the shadow of the cult of celebrity. Andy Warhol, the iconic pop artist, may have said 'in the future, everyone will be world famous for fifteen minutes' in 1968, but since he died in 1987, he really did not know the half of it. I wonder what he would have thought of reality television. Norah Jones, like the artists that Simphiwe is likened to above, points to the importance of making music of value, the kind that attracts critical acclaim rather than just sales.

Music occupies the realm of what really matters, as we hear these artists tell us again and again. Perhaps this is the 'message' that the stock South African radio caller yearns for in Chapter 7.

In interview after interview, it is clear that Simphiwe Dana values the distinction between being an artist and being someone who simply performs in the limelight. She does not apologise either for her craft or for the content of her lyrics, if it is even possible to think about them separately. It is important that she be recognised as 'an artist not an entertainer', as Peter quotes her saying. She says the same thing in the interview that accompanies her first DVD recording. In simple terms, Simphiwe is not interested in pretending to be something and someone that makes no sense to her. In this vein, given what the quotations from other artists above in this chapter say, it is clear that Peter does not choose her comparisons lightly. There is a family resemblance in how these artists think of themselves in relation to their craft and the larger musical world. For Dana, as she tells Peter and several others who interview her, including South African TV show host Penny Lebyane in an episode of the television series, *Motswako,* her vision is part of her craft, not a side issue. At the same time, Simphiwe is not unaware of the mixed responses she elicits. She argues that you need to know what you are doing, especially if you are a woman, and be quite assertive because in this industry people first tune into you because of your difference but they soon try to turn you into what they think makes sense. This is true even if responses to what she claims, argues and conjures are often at odds with her own sense of who she is in the world, as well as her value. It may surprise many that Simphiwe did not always know her own voice. She tells Masanda Peter that for a long time she wished to be a dancer, even though music was 'a secret passion' for her:

> I was embarrassed that I loved music so much that I wanted to pursue it as a career... I was never sure if I had a great voice. I never felt like Brenda Fassie, Miriam Makeba or Whitney Houston... One day I sang with a peer of mine at the school valedictory and my deputy principal told me I was a great singer. That was all I needed and those words changed my life and made me believe in myself.

Part of the difficulty Simphiwe had in initially giving herself permission to grasp at her musical dream was linked to the fact that most people around her recognised her mother's immense musical ability. As a daughter, Simphiwe could not imagine matching her mother's talent. This validation by her deputy principal is the vital confirmation of her suspicion that she is a talented musician in her own right. This deputy principal is most likely the music teacher she refers to in a different interview with Thando Pato, Mr Mniki, who tells Simphiwe after a performance with a friend, 'You know you could do this for a career'. And from that moment onwards, she is able to give herself permission to pursue her dream of living a life with music as one of its centres. In this instance, she has heard what she had not dared herself to think out loud. But the affirmation of an adult that she looks up to, who is knowledgeable, matters. She tells Pato:

> I really had respect for him because he'd travelled the world and I really listened to him. He was the first person to tell me that and it was all I needed because I thought I had a strange voice that was only good enough to sing in church. He confirmed what I felt inside and so I started planning my whole life around music. Even though I studied IT at university, my life is music.

Arriving in Johannesburg, it helped that she found a ready community of creative people working in different mediums to affirm her newfound identity as an artist and with whom she shared likes and politics. However, she does not romanticise this community. It was both an affirming space and one characterised by some difficulty. She is sometimes puzzled by the kinds of expectations placed on her as an artist. She notes how the recognition of what she brings to the table can both be appreciated one minute and met with the expectation that she will conform to some other standard desire at the same time. This apparent contradiction is due to her location in a contemporary South African reality that enables such transgressive artistic women, on the one hand, as Lebogang Mashile argues in an earlier chapter, whilst simultaneously producing powerful modes of policing conventional and unusual femininities. This tension speaks to a complex ambiguity – sometimes called the South African contradiction – that is both potentially inspiring for artistic creativity, but also crippling. This paradox may partly explain the complex responses to Simphiwe Dana that I discuss in this book.

In response to these expectations that she sees as really

outside herself, she says the following at different stages of her conversations with Peter:

You need to stick to your guns and as a woman you need to stand your ground.

My way of thinking is quite rare and I protect it.

I am where I had envisioned myself to be and do not feel that I have missed out on anything. People must keep up with me, as I am ahead of my time... I believe my ancestors are looking after me. It was their way of saying the Danas have been living in obscurity and it is their time to shine. I can now put the Dana surname on the map. I am humbled by all of this.

People do not like competition, but the type of talent I bring to the industry is different to what is already there. There is therefore no reason for other artists to feel threatened.

Sticking to her guns requires both confidence and conviction in her artistic vision. It relies on trusting herself even in the face of responses that question her at the same time as refusing to be drawn into unnecessary competition. This means she is able to feel fully, whether this is through experiencing the pleasure that flows from her choices or devastation. She is human, so I am not suggesting that she is unaffected emotionally by what people say about her and her music. But she is nobody's victim and she knows what she wants and because her commitment is to her craft and retaining musical integrity, she is able to defend her vision if needs be, or simply hold on to it.

This capacity is linked to the second statement about recognising that how she thinks, feels and sees the world is something precious and worthy of protection. As a result, she is able to plan her life in ways that make sense to her and not feel left out because of the choices she has made. It explains how she can make three magical, but radically different kinds of albums regardless of responses. But the third statement also shows something of the combination of Simphiwe's humour, wit and capacity to manage what seems mutually exclusive. She can recognise that she is exceptional without losing the sense of gratitude she calls humility.

And her success is verifiable in many ways. She embraces and questions these external measures at different times. But she is unflinching in her analysis and her right to speak her mind. Simphiwe's six South African Music Awards (SAMAs), her two Metro FM Awards as well as her numerous international music awards and her debut role as Mandisa in the feature film *Themba*, all demonstrate her creative range. She also speaks openly about having dreams about being a dancer in another life.

The accolades and nominations also support her larger sense of being both misunderstood and mostly ahead of her time. In her *Motswako* interview with Penny Lebyane, she confesses to being puzzled about the Metro FM Awards nominations given the fact that the radio station does not play her music. She recognises that her music and message are not always easy. She insists that she often feels unappreciated at home, but she stays because she does not want to be a coward.

She is not the kind of person who runs from her problems, on the one hand. South Africans, on the other hand, constantly choose to avert our gaze from our biggest challenges. Speaking about people not seeing her film on HIV/AIDS, she insists that South Africans do not want to deal with or directly address HIV/AIDS and other problems because they live the reality. Yet, for Simphiwe there is a contradiction and cowardice in not wanting to face your biggest challenges. She is her mother's daughter. She believes in confronting reality head on and giving yourself the capacity to deal with your reality. I do think that film distribution channels also have something to do with the relative invisibility of locally made feature films outside of the metropolitan centres. But it is possible to think about both these structural or infrastructural challenges and see merit in Simphiwe's argument about South Africans' reticence.

The above statements are not just what she says, however. They are blatantly obvious from some of her career choices. Her self-representation choices in her stage performances and music videos are very different from many other musicians in circulation. She is unafraid to develop her own visual vocabulary and language that is in step with the music she makes. It does not matter that producing shows and videos requires team work because what the team produces has to be in line with Simphiwe's vision. In several of her videos, an attentive viewer can pick up both an Afro-futuristic vision and traces of Simphiwe, the graphic designer. All of her videos are visually complex.

In her breakout hit '*Ndiredi*', the track that South Africans still want her to play at every concert even though other firm favourites have joined it, there are the juxtaposed faces of Simphiwe on several '60s-type television screens, a camera that shifts to a sleeping Simphiwe on a bed placed beneath a window that shows forms of multiplane, futuristic urban travel. Some of this is recognisable from our world: there are vehicles that resemble buses and trains in evolved form as well as spherical vehicles that look more like planets than means of transport. Alongside her bed, there is a blurred herb that could be *impepho*, *dagga* or *Kooigoed*. The screens tell us the date is 23/01/2017 but the monochrome screen announcing the news looks like an old fashioned DOS screen. The letters announce the impending alignment of stars in a six point star which has been much mythologised in religions throughout the world.

The metallic early Afro-futuristic aesthetic is sustained throughout this video when Simphiwe leaves her cabin and interacts with the physical and metaphysical world outside her bedroom and other women. All of these shifts make sense alongside Afro-futuristic musicians' previous fascination with both the racism-free utopic future and examining the past. This flirtation with Afro-futurism is also evident in the styling of the jacket covers of her first and third CDs. However, by the third CD, Simphiwe is interested in a different stage on the Afro-futuristic continuum. In her 2009 video for the track 'One Love Movement on Bantu

Biko Street,' she visually journeys backwards to the sepia-toned era also symbolised by the nurse's uniform Simphiwe wears in the video. But the fantasy aspect is still present in the iridescent pieces of paper that she collects as though they are treasures for insertion into a glass jar she carries throughout when dressed as a nurse as well as in the disappearing homeless woman figure who pushes a trolley on which sits a planet aglow.

Her videos are as visually saturated with meaning and as layered as her lyrics. Regardless of the very specific registers that she chooses for different videos, her characters are constantly moving, searching, travelling through different dimensions of existence – through walls, streets, forests, water, planets. In her visual language, there is always the suggestion that boundaries can be broken down and moved through, that they are as permanent or as fluid as the imaginative capacity of those they seek to contain. She is not escapist, though. It is not as though the boundaries are not there, whether visually or in her other work where she challenges the limitations placed by violent power. It is a refusal to accept boundaries. Patricia McFadden asserts 'I REFUSE to obey any and all forms of patriarchal supremacy, and I will continue to spurn such conceited, patriarchal injunctions.' There is something of what Simphiwe does in this statement. It is not that she exists *outside* of patriarchal limitation. It is that she is constantly pushing the limits of what is possible, even what she has previously thought possible. This requires risk, and all risk comes with harm some of the time. Sometimes the harm is simply being wrong.

In her videos, Simphiwe is not the sexually appealing object of the viewer's gaze that we find in so many music videos today. Instead, she constantly opts for a different kind of presence as a singer, writer and performer. Her body is part of what she uses to communicate in these videos. Her video colour palette is dark or off-colour. She steers clear of the polished, heavily contrasted effect of many mainstream videos. At the same time, Simphiwe's videos are able to elegantly marry very serious visual vocabulary with fun and discovery, again echoing what she was saying about who she is in her 2007 *True Love* interview. They are a pleasure to watch, and often perform pleasure. Even the sombre 'State of Emergency' video is visually beautiful. Her body is present in each video: dancing, sitting, thinking. She is often in community but her body is hers in all her videos; she is never accessory, owned or confined. She presents a radically different reality of women's presences than we see often in South African popular culture, and indeed, in every single video from her first three albums, she presents the connotations of rebellion as rewarding and pleasurable. There is no disciplined body. The body that appears again and again moves through space, emotion on the face, changes clothes.

Visually, there is a very clear sense in which a fantasy is at play in both what is evaded and what is achieved, suggested. Her visual presence mirrors exactly what she says about her place in the production of her art, what she says, what she believes about art as well as what she does not want. There are clear synergies between her spoken intention and her practice musically, as well as in the products themselves. She is not defiant of patriarchal conventional femininity in her videos. She simply does not engage it. Her project and interest lies elsewhere because she imagines something else. In many respects, to speak about her as defying some of these femininities is to insult and limit what she really *creates*.

There is also the sense of her determination in her videos where she both interacts with others and walks alone. This is not something new. She is both a woman who needs to make her way through the world, and one who is aware that she can. She tells Masanda Peter:

> I did not grow up with my parents, but was rather raised by my grandparents and therefore I have been self-reliant since I was a young girl... Our house was headed by a woman, which is not a unique situation. Through that experience I realised that no woman should themselves [sic] for a man leaving her. Pity that as long as we have too many of those kinds of households we will have another generation like that. My mother has been my rock. I wrote the song *Chula ukunyathela (Take it easy)* for her. I want her to take it easy

and we will work for her now. She is my best friend as I do not have many friends in the industry.

Simphiwe's voice softens when she speaks about her mother. She writes songs for her, is protective of her and admires her mother's efforts as well as the kind of woman she is. She is clearly proud of her mother as she relates her resilience, sacrifices, and her capacity to remake herself from domestic worker to nurse. This, Simphiwe's feminism, is a model of feminism akin to a definition that Arundhati Roy provides in her novel, *The God of Small Things*: A feminist is a woman who negotiates herself into a position where she has choices.

Although the model of domesticity discussed earlier in this chapter constrains family and intimacy so that it can only be recognised when it fits into specific parameters, Simphiwe is as unconstrained in the ways she loves as she is in the ways she lives. In her very public relationship with Hessel Pole, she found – and later lost – love. It was a meeting of spirits that she talked about openly. She shared a *True Love* magazine spread and cover with him, and later told South African TV presenter Penny Lebyane on *Motswako* of her utter joy in finding him when she did. She spoke about him as 'The One' who helped her rediscover love just as she emerged out of a difficult period brought on, in part, by the near total silent response to her second album. But this great romance, not her first or last, also required her to shift some of her behaviours, as love sometimes does. She was pleasantly surprised by it and made no apologies for her enjoyment of it.

Some people argue that it endangers a relationship to expose it to the public in this way. They insist that relationships should be protected and treasured. But these same people walk around hand-in-hand with the people they love, speak openly about their feelings. They seldom say this to people speaking about their husbands or wives. They often say it to people with public lives who are not married. I think there is freedom in living your life openly, with scant regard to what society says is appropriate. It is a strange and unfair expectation to ask someone to hide who they love. Because Simphiwe is so determined to live her life on her terms – even though this is not always possible – she did the opposite of what such advice suggests. In her *New African Woman* interview with Masanda Peter, she enthused:

> I have someone in my life who completely adores me and is very understanding... As far as romance is concerned, I grew up in a conservative home and I have hence been a bit reserved. But my man, who is of African-American descent, is teaching me to come out of my shell and discover my sexuality. He loves my body, and he is the love of my life. I would like to make the relationship permanent because I know he is the one. After breaking up with the father of my two kids I did not want to introduce them to men in my life. Strangely enough, within two weeks my kids were calling him 'daddy'. I was scared he was going to leave me, leaving my children heartbroken when they became attached but the relationship is going strong. When I am travelling, he usually takes care of my children.

She took a risk on love. Like her, I think that love is worth the risk. Arundhati Roy seems to agree with us, when she writes the following in *The Cost of Living*:

> The only dream worth having is to dream that you will live while you are alive, and die only when you are dead. To love, to be loved. To never forget your own insignificance. To never get used to the unspeakable violence and vulgar disparity of the life around you. To seek joy in the saddest places. To pursue beauty to its lair. To never simplify what is complicated or complicate what is simple. To respect strength, never power. Above all to watch. To try and understand. To never look away. And never, never to forget.

While we agree with Roy's statement, we also disagree about what it means to live as she describes. In other words, Simphiwe's and my own feminisms often express themselves very differently from each other. Our biggest disagreements in this respect have thus far been on commitment and sexual expression.

Although we both identify as feminists, nowhere is our disagreement more evident than in our political stances on multiple partnerships. Simphiwe's stance on polygamy can be crystallised into the following statements:

In practice polygamy doesn't favour women.

I've made mistakes. And they must stay as that, mistakes. Institutionalising them would make a poorer person of me.

Polygamy is institutionalized cheating and it seems to favour men.

The last statement was framed with the proviso that although she would respect and entertain the possibility of polygamy – expressed as polyandry, polygamy and a combination – if we lived in a non-patriarchal society, the society we live in renders her support impossible. Consequently, she would neither be a polygamist nor want to think about being in any intimate association with one.

I both agree and disagree with her stance on polygamy. I have currently neither the desire for multiple simultaneous committed partnerships nor the desire to be one of several lovers or partners for a specific *man* within a serious relationship. However, I think of sexuality as a continuum, not just in terms of sexual orientation, but also in terms of desire. I also recognise that different human beings identify and desire different things from the ones I am interested in. There is a problem in prescribing my own, current preference as the most, or exclusively, legitimate one. This normalises me, but always runs the risk of marking other people's desires as abnormal. There isn't something implicitly desirable about monogamy any more than there is anything implicitly undesirable about multiple concurrent partnerships – as long as there is honesty on both fronts.

There is at the same time a problem with prescribing my own personal preference as the norm and using it to then automatically disqualify all those who choose differently from me, especially on the grounds of how patriarchy works. Where I stand, heterosexual marriage is one of patriarchy's central institutions. Most marriages, even, or especially, when they are monogamous, are by default patriarchal. The only time marriage is not patriarchal is when it is made non-patriarchal. The argument for polygamous marriages as patriarchal, *which they are*, should not be made in a way that claims that monogamous marriages are freer, because they are not. Most married people are in monogamous marriages, and most of those marriages are patriarchal because our very conception of what marriage is requires very rigid gender roles, even in a society such as ours where public gender discourse and paperwork can be so transgressive. So, I can only agree with Simphiwe's statement that polygamy disadvantages women because default heterosexual marriage does not 'favour women'. To this, I would add that polygyny specifically favours men.

Many of the most heavily defended aspects of marriage enshrine a racialised, class-marked patriarchy: *lobola*, engagement rings, white wedding dresses after Queen Victoria, being walked up the aisle by the father-figure to be handed over to the groom, chivalry, the proposal on bended knee by the man, the veiled bride, *ukuyalwa*, *ukwembeswa*, the kinds of gifts exchanged at *amabhaso* and kitchen teas, the differences between parties for the bride and groom to be prior to the wedding, the asymmetry in what is expected from a daughter-in-law versus what is expected from a son-in-law *vis a vis* dress and service to the families people marry into, sexual and reproductive expectations, labour and childcare expectations, the changing of surname and the surname taken on by the offspring in marriage.

There is nothing automatically feminist about either monogamous or polygamous relationships. Women will choose relationships with differing degrees of choice given that we live in a patriarchal and therefore unequal world. Not all women are feminist. No oppressive system has ever succeeded without the complicity and active support of members of those classes/groups it seeks to oppress. This is part of why the personal is political.

Feminists have been arguing that monogamous heterosexual families are very often at the heart of patriarchal exploitation of women's sexual, emotional, economic, psychological, reproductive and intellectual labour for a long time. Homes are both sites of affirmation and battlegrounds because they are always affected by power expressed through race, class, sexual orientation, religion, gender or geography. Most women experience rape and other forms of violence from their intimate male partners in formally monogamous contexts, so it is dangerous to romanticise marriage based on how many people are in it. Like many feminists I see conventional monogamous marriage as that which is about controlling women, containing women's sexual desire, and policing women's reproduction.

African feminists especially have said that most monogynous heterosexual relationships benefit the man (to put it mildly) at the expense of the woman in it, but also that multiple partner relationships can be about much more than oppression. Some feminists say the institution of marriage is inherently patriarchal. Lola Shoneyin's beautiful novel *The Secret Lives of Baba Segi's Wives* demonstrates this complexity very well. In it, Shoneyin portrays women who have different kinds of relationships with each other. The co-wives are sometimes competitive, as can be expected. They are also supportive of each other and realise similarities with each other in a range of unpredictable ways. One of these ways centres around how they all have lovers in addition to their shared husband. They marry him for very different reasons, and once they all choose to stop engaging with each other in competitive ways, each of the co-wives enjoys the protection of the others. Their lovers are wide-ranging, even if this knowledge is protected from a new wife, until the newest wife finally finds herself enamoured by someone outside the circle. In other words, Shoneyin suggests that it is only when women focus their sexual and romantic energies solely on their shared husband that the relationships are tense and difficult. In Shoneyin's magical novel, when women focus on a range of possibilities for themselves, including the possibility of non-exclusive partnership, they are less hostile to other women.

Competition for the main man fuels aggression. This African feminist poet and novelist's vision of women's sexuality that unsettles the primacy of the husband can be quite scary for those of us brought up on the diet of heterosexual monogamy as the ultimate prize. Yet, Shoneyin's vision is refreshing in its refusal to dictate or demonise women's desires, in the writer's refusal to subjugate women's relationship with other women to their relationships to men, and in her resistance to romanticise either monogamy or polygamy.

Outside of her novel, the scapegoating of polygamy allows us to look away from how messy the logic of romance is everywhere, even within exclusive monogamous relationships. It is important to expose the lie that monogamy translates to exclusivity. Indeed the competition for a man in order to marry encourages multiple partnerships even in spaces where men declare one primary relationship.

Therefore, the stress should be less on one kind of marriage being bad and another being good, and more on widening the capacity of people to choose what they desire openly and in non-gender-rigid ways. Many who support polygamy support the patriarchal sense of entitlement men in our society are raised to feel towards women and our bodies. For them polygamy is simply an extension of one man, many women (polygyny), even though they would reject the same options being presented to women (polyandry). They believe that a man with multiple women lovers is a playboy, *isoka* and a woman who has multiple men as lovers is a 'whore'. When they say polygamy, they mean specifically polygyny. Polyandry does not even enter the equation and when it is brought up, it is decried as permission for women to be whores. The fact that some of the partners and lovers women desire might themselves be women or transgendered people does not even enter the public debate that habitually explodes around 'polygamy' in South Africa. In a sense, then, I agree with Simphiwe that *in practice*, in the current limited patriarchal and heterosexist application, *polygamy doesn't favour women*. However, I disagree that the solution is policing desire. In principle, women who wish to be free from full-time devotion to one man should be able to choose polyamorous combinations of different kinds without the stigma.

But the patriarchal opportunism that Simphiwe rejects is real. All the people who are saying 'it is my culture' to practice polygamy mean it is their culture for a man to have many women as partners – polygyny. They are also saying that their culture is static and we should all respect it without question, even if and when it speaks for us too. They also ignore the inconvenient point that women are the majority of any 'culture' and therefore cannot be completely precluded from defining its contents.

But, as feminists, we insist that if it is ours too, then we can change, lay claim to it, question how it is being misrepresented. Every single proponent of the 'culture' plus 'polygamy' argument that I have read in the South African news, seen or personally debated on radio, television or new media platforms has refused the same courtesy to women with multiple partners, whether these partners be men, women, intersex and/or trans-people, or a combination. So, they are saying 'it is my culture to practice polygamy' but what they mean is 'it is my culture to enter into polygyny'. And there is nothing specifically African about polygamy – people all over the world choose and reject it. Officially and unofficially people enter into polyamorous situations all the time, and usually in dishonest ways. This is also part of the family script, linked to the expectations on women's sexuality governed by domesticity.

As Tamale reminds us, however, domesticity is also about parenting in specific ways and passing on the script of domesticity to those we parent directly and indirectly. We see Simphiwe's feminist insistence in the choices she makes about parenting as well, some of which are hinted at in her comments on her partnership with Hessel, above. Parenting is about taking care of children in affirming, loving and freeing ways and can be undertaken by men, women and transgender people. It is a social activity that need not be undertaken only in the presence of blood ties.

When Simphiwe speaks about parenting, she stresses that she does not want to limit her children. This is also very clear in how she parents them, her decisions about where to place the boundaries they need in order to have structure, support and affirmation in their lives. At the same time, she does give them enormous freedom to express and pursue their desires and inner selves. She is unromantic about both her parenting choices and the way in which she was parented:

> My kids are going to assume roles that are not gender specific. I want them both to feel equal.

> My mother was married to my father but he did not play his role as a father. He was around and did not have time for us. Sadly, I do not have much of a relationship with him.

Finally, what analysing different facets of Simphiwe's desire – or 'desirings', as human being, a woman, an artist – in this chapter, as a manifestation of her soft feminism has shown is that her soft feminism is, in fact, everywhere. It permeates how she chooses to represent herself, the ways in which she negotiates what is private and public.

She is a woman who consistently lives outside the parameters of idealised femininities in South Africa, and the world, but at the same time she is painstakingly honest about her flirtation with aspects of idealised femininity. She does not pretend to be immune to certain desires that come with being brought up as a girl in a patriarchal world that pretends that we are all heterosexual, in perpetual pursuit of a husband and a stable family-life. But her life choices suggest that she is not willing to be trapped by any single narrative of love, parenting, femininity or desire. She reserves the right to change her mind, alter previous behaviour and shift in ways that retain integrity. As a soft feminist, she will not live her life on a stage, soaking up the approval and adoration. Rather, she continues to protect what she yearns for and her 'way of thinking', allowing it to grow, and in ways that enable her to expand the range of choices available to her – and other people.

CHAPTER 5

Love, language and anguish

To *alienate a child from its home language is nothing short of abuse.*

Ngugi wa Thiong'o

Mastery of language affords remarkable power.

Frantz Fanon

Why would a country battling the effects of centuries of oppression allow this? Wouldn't language be the focal point in our struggle for the cultural emancipation of our mangled identity?

Simphiwe Dana

At the end of October 2010, Simphiwe Dana published an op-ed in the *Sunday Times* bemoaning the dire state of language education and access in post-apartheid South Africa. Titling her piece 'Let's agree on Zulu as our first language; at least it's African', Simphiwe introduced the piece in the following way:

The year is over and I am reminded of the pain I felt at the beginning of this year when I was looking for schools for my children. I am based in Cape Town, but I found it impossible to get them into a good school not far from home that offered an African language as part of the curriculum. Now, I am not talking about a third language as is the norm in these previously model C schools. I was looking for a school that offered Xhosa as a first language.

Given the state of public education, many parents who would ordinarily have chosen to put their children in public school institutions as a deliberate political decision now realise that with a collapsing school system, that is tantamount to deliberately setting their children up for future failure. For those parents who can afford the astronomical cost of private school education, it is the only way to guarantee some semblance of quality education. South African novelist and essayist Zukiswa Wanner has noted that:

If it doesn't sound too simplistic, it's clear to me from my investigation that the problem of the South African education system is political: the politics of language and the politics of class mixed up in the country's unfortunate historical circumstances which continue to haunt its citizens.

The levels of public debate on the appalling state of South African education both under apartheid as well as in the last eighteen years of democracy proceed parallel to the continuing degeneration of the public schooling system, rather than in conversation. When she travelled throughout South Africa as part of a project that investigated various aspects of the South African education system, Zukiswa Wanner offered the following comments, drawn from her reflections on that field research:

Ask any South African resident observer what they feel the greatest failing of their nation has been post the first democratic elections of 1994 and chances are that half your respondents will mention education.

As a parent, I am certainly not one of those who advocate use of English at the expense of the mother tongue. Indeed, my six-year-old son speaks passable isiXhosa and has an impressive understanding of his grandmother's language, Karanga. I take umbrage with parents who say proudly 'My son/daughter only speaks English', or '*Yhu!* Your child speaks English so well'.

For both Simphiwe and Zukiswa Wanner, the education system invites feelings of sadness and panic. The collapse of the education system is avoidable but not avoided.

Let me then return extensively to Simphiwe's *Sunday Times* piece, which proved quite provocative in terms of the larger discussion it elicited in the media and on social networks. Because I think this op-ed has many more layers and implications than the responses picked up on, I want to spend some time spelling out what Simphiwe's arguments are in that piece.

First, Simphiwe points out that in much of urban South Africa, outside of townships, looking for schools that teach indigenous African languages is a lesson in pain. She refers to this in the two events she lists as shaping her experience of looking for a suitable school for her children in Cape Town. I am pretty sure that she has had similar experiences in Johannesburg because several prominent media examples have highlighted how fraught the indigenous language teaching situation is in South African schools.

This dire situation is true because only English and Afrikaans, out of eleven official languages of the country, are consistently taught in ways that take the language seriously and in a manner that encourages language acquisition and usage at first language competency levels.

Simphiwe then links the problems with the current language and education landscape with the disadvantages of such poor indigenous language teaching. She argues that the status of a people's language is a good indication of the collective status of those people's culture and cultural outlook. But this second aspect it not as simple as it first seems. Dana argues the following two points with regard to status:

> We are pathetic versions of our colonial masters. No wonder we are so apologetic about the continued suppression of our identity, of our culture, our languages. How can we expect to evolve our culture when we are caught in this state of mind? If our languages die, we only have ourselves to blame.
>
> Language is the bringer of culture. What we have forgotten of ourselves is hidden in our African languages. Language might be the revolution Africa needs. I say this because the biggest success apartheid had was making us unsure of ourselves. If I go home and am among people who speak my language, an African language, I feel more sure of myself. If our former colonisers want to reconcile, they must rally behind this cause, this understanding, that this is Africa, and in Africa African culture rules.

Language was used to oppress, wound and marginalise. This is why we have different appreciation of languages that have a discernible connection with Europe, and a marginalisation of languages that are indigenous to Africa. Exclusion from a language of this place is also a psychic and conceptual exclusion, not just the inability to communicate in another language. If we take the reconciliation possibility seriously as South Africans, one of the key areas in which thinking needs to radically shift is that of language.

At the same time, Simphiwe questions what it means that even though Black people have political and legal power in a democratic South Africa, we allow our languages to remain marginal, available in the school system only to the most marginal of South African children who live in township and rural areas and go to public schools. Why should we have to take our children to township schools for them to learn languages that are indigenous to this country and continent? she asks. Parents should not have to move or take their children to township schools in order to have their language – which is their right legally – taken and taught seriously.

In any event, this migration to townships has the effect of re-inscribing the narrative that Black people belong to the peripheries. Simphiwe's stance on this is captured in her song 'Sizophum'eLokishini' from the album *One Love Movement on Bantu Biko Street*, which insists that it is time to leave the townships, the places of madness and reservoirs of tears rather than the gold 'we' came to mine. This song is a call to urgently leave the townships. But the townships are both the geographical ghettos that have come to define 'authentic' Blackness and the mentality that polices legitimate forms of Blackness. Townships are a white supremacist construction, and although they have been shaped by vibrancy, defiance and counter-cultures, the time to claim the world beyond township borders has long been with us. The song is both a call to leave and an assertion that this will happen. It is a defiant attention to history, a love song to Biko who 'raises' her and gives her the tools through which to push for change. But the addressee is not just the implied Biko for whom this project is named. It is also Black people in general. The song is in different turns reflective, consoling and motivating a significant mindset and physical response.

She insists that language is important for healing as well as for a connection to the past that is not about romanticising historic greatness. In other words, all South Africans should have access to at least one indigenous language within the formal support of the school system as well as beyond. She suggests that the specific African language learnt is less important than the actual process of learning it and benefitting from the worldview it offers. For Dana, while there is attachment to home language, any of the African languages available to us in South Africa will do. She chooses Zulu for practical reasons.

The choice of one common language is informed by the argument that languages from the same place offer the same kind of philosophical-conceptual-spiritual framework. African languages, she argues, carry more than the meanings in the words used to communicate. They carry a worldview and a series of abstract and concrete reference points that are present in various African languages.

I agree that this is always true of language. This is why even those of us who are polyglots often cannot translate a concept across unrelated language families. This is also why I have said over and over again that I would prefer to send my child to a school that teaches all South African languages on its books at first language level. I am not overly concerned about whether the language is Xitsonga or isiZulu or Sesotho. Like Simphiwe, I am not overly concerned about which indigenous African language is the school's choice as long as it is taught well. This is an urgent task that we must take up or deal with the consequences of language neglect.

At the same time, I would prefer my child to be *also* fluent in isiXhosa and Sesotho, because these are the home languages of my birth family. It is simply impractical to expect my nuclear and extended families to speak to my child in English all the time. It is far from both desirable and practical. I would also like my child to be able to read at a literary and conceptual level in his mother tongues. If we were not all apologetic about claiming entitlement to the formal educational recognition of our languages because of the ever-present haunting of ethnic nationalism, I suspect that this issue would have been addressed, especially since it overwhelmingly affects middle-class Black children. It has taken me a long time to be able to accept labelling as Xhosa, not just as Black and African. Although I would like to pretend that this is exclusively due to the Black Consciousness positive identification as Black (which I embrace), when I am being honest with myself, I have to admit that I am battling on *how* to claim that identity whilst at the same time signalling a distance from the Xhosa ethnic nationalists of my youth, the monstrous ghosts of homeland leaders Lennox Sebe and Kaiser Matanzima, presidents, respectively, of the two antagonistic, but equally ethnic nationalist Ciskei and Transkei Bantustans, and their crew.

In my academic work, I think about multiple belongings and the untidiness of identity not as crisis-inducing, but as a fact of life.

And I take the multiple languages spoken by members of both sides of my family as a source of great pride. Yet, there is much about Xhosa and Sotho belonging, history and languages that is joyful, pride-inducing, pleasurable and instructive. It does not all belong to the homeland folk, their sell-out politics and their violence, and my journey to be able to claim both identities together and separately has required an acceptance of this. But when I speak to many Black South African friends of my generation, my squeamishness about being Xhosa is echoed in how there were different sections in Chiawelo township, Johannesburg as they grew up, or how they were so-called coloured growing up and are certainly not interested in being Coloured now. However, as Simphiwe notes, if we raise a generation of children who cannot speak any African languages, then it will be on us.

Often, the only schools that do this are schools whose other values are at odds with mine. It is an odd choice to have to make for a child's education between sending your child to a school that takes his language and his right to language seriously but also inculcates consumer capitalist values, on the one hand, and one with a reputation for progressive politics but that tells him his language, ancestry and continent are expendable on the other. Fortunately, this is not a choice I have had to make.

Simphiwe's motivation for choosing isiZulu as the shared adopted African language is that it is already widely spoken and relatively easy on the tongue. But she realises that even if her resolve is shared, this is not a reality that will evolve into being. Rather, she asserts that we need to hold our current government responsible and accountable for the language mess in our schools even as we keep an eye on the historical contexts that brought us here.

Her final point pertains to how she defines the parameters of what constitutes an African language. This is a category that excludes English and Afrikaans for her. She argues that Afrikaans is not an African language because it carries the arrogance of the Dutch colonisers and the apartheid establishment. Although the language was shaped through African location, its Afrikaner nationalist use ensured that it remained a language of wounding, rather than one which made itself at home. The phrasing that comes to mind to describe the phenomenon Simphiwe describes here is, strangely, from South African writer JM Coetzee's study of white literature called *White Writing* where he argues that this is a literature by people 'no longer European, not yet African'. Simphiwe's conceptualisation of Afrikaans is suited to this definition. I say strange because neither Simphiwe nor I are particularly enamoured of Coetzee's creative work.

I have spent some time spelling out Simphiwe's argument in the *Sunday Times* op-ed because I think it raises important concerns. It raises several issues that need to be raised again and again until something changes. The bulk of the responses in the media were defensive, but I am not overly concerned with them here. Anybody who writes an op-ed about Black marginalisation in any arena in South Africa elicits this kind of silencing. Some of the responses were the usual ones about the chip on her shoulder, accusations of playing victim and the 'race card', as well as that she did not know what she was talking about. Some took it upon themselves to educate her on how out of touch she was with what matters in the world and the country, that most Black parents do not mind the condescending third language level taught at Model C schools because children need to speak English to make it in the world.

There was the favourite phrase of English as 'an international language' thrown in too as part of the demonstrated contempt for African ways of being.

Another strand of responses wilfully misread her in a different direction, claiming that it is important to move on from a fascination with African languages. This argument was made by Black people who claim radical leftist political affiliation at the same time that they uncritically argue for a Black modern subjectivity. Such subjectivity cannot be bothered with romantic notions of African languages, identities and worldviews and it is overly anxious about the appearance of ethnic nationalism.

Thus, while Simphiwe pre-empted some of these in the careful way in which she articulated her argument, showing the benefits of African language fluency as well as her political rather than nostalgic ethnicist motivation, the responses appeared predetermined.

I value Simphiwe's decision to speak on this difficult topic because she also had to have known the tenor of some of the responses. She was to receive much more hateful responses to later public stances.

She is correct in her reading of the state of language education in many South African schools post-apartheid. The reality she accurately describes is an insult of the highest order for the children who go to such schooling, regardless of what race they are. South African children should be able to speak various languages in their country – more than their parents can, even when their parents are polyglots. The school system should play a leading role in this, but it is instead directly implicated in maintaining the status quo.

I was not surprised when I read her article. This is a topic that had come up several times in conversations with other parents in my own life. I was aghast, when my former life partner and I started looking at possible schools for our child, to learn that most schools we would have preferred – many with progressive credentials – teach English and Afrikaans at first language level, and any other chosen official language at third language level until the end of primary school. This is not even sound education practice, given that human beings have the greatest capacity to learn language in the first six years of life.

But I also have a few friends who took isiXhosa third language at school, and although they all passed it well in the school leaving examinations, Matric, none of them can have a conversation in the language. None of them can speak isiXhosa beyond tentative understanding and elementary small talk. Learning to speak a language at third language level does not teach you how to speak it no matter what your grades say. Simphiwe writes:

A third language is not functional as it provides only a very basic form of communication – what an employer would need in order to pass on instructions to an illiterate servant, while never truly understanding the servant's language.

The fact that languages are taught at third language level at all is an insult. It is a practice that keeps indigenous languages marginal. It makes a joke of the eleven-language policy and legislation since it is only true on paper. It also points to the inefficiency of our own government on this point as well as – perhaps more so – the irresponsibility of the parents who continue to leave this unchallenged in the schools they pay fees to.

The current situation means that while these schools are located in a democracy, they effectively operate as though they are in an apartheid state with two official languages. Active citizenship requires the constant contestation of this norm. Ntombenhle Nkosi's example to litigate is one that we should pursue more readily, as reported in the *Mail and Guardian* article 'Durban school taught "kitchen" Zulu' in the 28 July 2008 issue of the weekly newspaper. At the time of the court case, Nkosi was the Chief Executive Officer (CEO) of the Pan South African Language Board (PANSALB). She argued that the level at which her son was taught isiZulu at a Durban private school was well below par with English and Afrikaans tuition at the same school. Nkosi insisted that this effectively discriminated against her son and other similarly-placed children.

The Equality Court magistrate John Sanders, hearing the case in Durban, noted that 'the scenario falls squarely within the definition of discrimination in terms of the Equality Act', as reported by Wonder Hlongwa in 'Parent wins school language battle in court', published in *City Press* on 30 September 2008. In the same article, Ms Nkosi pointed to how widespread such discrimination was, and argued for the allocation of state financial resources so that 'inspectors could be appointed to check whether learners were being discriminated against in schools'. The PANSALB CEO and litigant's statement to the reporter outside the court rhymed with the magistrate's statement while passing judgement. Magistrate Sanders insisted that 'every single school in KwaZulu-Natal should be fully equipped to teach isiZulu at LLC1 (highest) level of tuition', rather than the current LLC3, which is the lowest level of language tuition.

Quoted in the *Sowetan* (2 October 2008) after her victory, Nkosi noted:

> Parents must just not take it for granted that schools are going to do it for them, they won't. Every parent must ensure that their language – be it isiXhosa, be it isiSwati, Zetswane, Sesotho Saleboa, Tshivenda, Tsonga – must be offered as the first language because the National Curriculum Statement states that every learner must choose the home language, not the home language of the school.

I will say nothing of the typos in the transcribed quotation, even though they, too, tell an interesting story about the disrespect of African languages. Nor was Nkosi's case isolated to KZN Province, as is clear from the East London story of another parent, Ayanda Duma 'and at least 200 other Gonubie parents', who took Gonubie Primary School to the Equality Court for choosing to offer only Afrikaans as an additional first language for students in 2012.

In 'Parents in race row over isiXhosa', Sabelo Skiti, writing for *City Press* on 28 April 2012, noted the insidious ways in which isiXhosa was taken out of the running through the election of a school governing body composed exclusively out of white parents, in a school where there are either '400 Xhosa, 200 English and 70 Afrikaans' mother tongue pupils at the school or '387, 400 and 32, respectively'. The disputed numbers belong to the litigants and the school, respectively. Ms Duma is quoted as saying:

> My husband and I made a conscious decision to move back from Pretoria to the Eastern Cape in 2008 so that our children can learn to speak and be taught in their mother tongue, but now the school is sidelining us.

Realising that expecting their children to be taught first language isiXhosa might be tricky in Gauteng, these parents moved to a province where the vast majority of inhabitants are Xhosa mother tongue speakers. The Dumas were not as successful as Nkosi, however, due to a range of missing pieces of the legislative puzzle in the Eastern Cape province.

In 'New rights for first languages', Msindisi Fengu, writing in the *Daily Dispatch's* 8 October 2012 edition highlights various other complications in this regard. A Language Bill was still being drafted which would enable parents to effectively take on cases such as Duma's. Currently, Fengu's interviews with assistant manager in the Eastern Cape Department of Sports, Recreation, Arts and Culture language section, Mcoseleli Dukisa and Education Member of Executive Council (MEC), Mandla Makupula, showed that 'there was no legislation to support Ayanda Duma's case' and that 'senior officials in [Makupula's] department were afraid to intervene into language policy matters at former Model C schools'.

The absence of a framework that enables the Duma family to have the same legal recourse as Nkosi is a tragedy and a travesty. Undeterred, Ayanda Duma took the matter to court, and in the article, 'Mom wins equality for Xhosa at school', published in the *Daily Dispatch* on 25 January 2013, Msindi Fengu reported on Ayanda Duma's success in forcing Gonubie Primary School to offer Xhosa at first language level.

I do, however, have some disagreements with aspects of Simphiwe's argument, although I do so mostly on technicalities. First, although I want my child to be taught an African language as a first language at school, alongside English, I am not convinced that our children need to learn only *one* such language. Many Model C schools are capable of teaching children how to speak German and French alongside English and Afrikaans. With motivation, they are capable of doing the same with African languages.

I also disagree that isiZulu is easier than other indigenous languages because there is no such thing as a universally easy language. What is easy for a learner is determined by that learner's prior knowledge. This would then suggest that while isiZulu might be easier for a Ndebele or Xhosa speaker, than Xitsonga, it will not necessarily be easier for a Venda speaker.

The third point of disagreement is around the adoption of a language spoken by a larger group due to issues of future language dominance. We are automatically saying something about how we value Tshivenda or Xitsonga differently when we make a numerically dominant language like isiZulu or isiXhosa more appropriately official. We do not matter because there are many of us. We matter because we are human beings.

My final point is around the value we attach to Afrikaans. Unlike Simphiwe, I argue that Afrikaans *is* an African language, although I would agree that it is not one in the same linguistic and cosmological sense that Sepedi is. Afrikaans comes from a range of languages and was formed as a creole in the mouths of slaves. The first texts written in Afrikaans were not written by people who were 'Dutch' – the first Afrikaans texts were written in Arabic script because that was the script used by the first Muslims in the Cape, many of whom came as slaves from the East African hinterland, East African islands, South Asia and South East Asia. This makes Afrikaans not Dutch any more than Caribbean creole languages are English or kiSwahili Arabic. At the same time, once defiled by the Dutch, this creole then became appropriated for Afrikaner nationalism in a manner that ensured that it could be used against the very people whose ancestors formed it and were punished for speaking it.

Yes, someone who speaks Nederlands may understand parts of Afrikaans, and parts of Aukan (a Surinamese creole also formed by slaves using partly Dutch). However, Aukan is not Afrikaans is not Dutch, even if we do not dispute that they are related. At the same time, to say Afrikaans is African does not undo the fact that Afrikaans is *also* the language of wounding, misrecognition, displacement, oppression, apartheid. To honour part of our African ancestry we must remember the former because it was their mouths that crafted the creole and were punished for speaking it. To honour another part of our African ancestry, we must highlight the latter. For most Black South Africans growing up under apartheid, Afrikaans was the latter. For many Black South Africans (especially some classified 'coloured'), it was both. This is our thorny inheritance, and it all matters.

The language problem is not simply one of schooling and

education, however. Interestingly, in June 2007, I had written an op-ed on language for the *Mail and Guardian* as well as a blog entry. In the latter, I had reflected on the ironies of celebrating another anniversary of the 16 June 1976 uprisings given the state of education for most youth. I wrote:

> Language also continues to be fraught terrain for most of us largely due to economic reasons. I would love to be able to do all my banking in isiXhosa, or get served in Sesotho, or hear an entire airline announcement – not just the tokenistic greeting – in isiZulu. Instead, in this arena as in others, the glorious framework provided by national legislation notwithstanding, the only information and documentation that is routinely and regularly available in the eleven official languages is government information. I am thinking of withholding support and money from companies that continue to use only English and Afrikaans in interfacing with all clients. Sometimes the only language that works for corporate is money. What a shoddy legacy for the class of 1976. What bizarre inaction for those of them alive and working in provincial government, in charge of teacher salaries and with clout in corporate!

I am well aware that I might well starve if I cease to do business with companies that only work in English and Afrikaans. At the same time, I am reminded of that poster that used to make the rounds in the 1990s where hundreds of thousands of people stand in a square, inactive, all individually thinking 'what can one person do?'

When I returned to the topic again, I partly answered the question in the poster, but without clear resolution for all the language problems I had articulated above. I wrote:

> A friend visiting from Sierra Leone once nodded in agreement with a Nigerian colleague's comment: "the great thing about South Africa is that you really value your languages".

She had asked me what language *Generations* or *Isidingo* characters were speaking to each other, finding it remarkable that national television used more than one language in this way: evidence of a linguistically complex democracy.

I cringed. If only this were applicable to more than visionary SABC television broadcasts. They have recognised that in our homes we like being spoken to like we matter. Lest the SABC be made to seem exceptional, let me point to another example of similar respect for the millions of people who call this country home: the organisation, translate.org, an organisation with a miniscule fraction of the budget of most corporate entities. Translate.org has translated an entire electronic office suite into the eleven official languages, and anybody can download whichever ones they want for free from their site and distribute them freely and legally at will.

I cringed at the offered compliment because thirteen years into a complicated democracy, these organisations are almost alone in this regard. The discomfort was familiar.

Every few months, the email about Black South Africa's fraught relationship to language lands in one of my inboxes. We speak English all day, conduct business exclusively in English, do most of our writing – even to relatives and those with whom we share African languages – in English, and sometimes speak to our children predominantly in English. We say it just makes things easier. There are no easily accessible equivalent words in an indigenous African language, we claim. But why do we leave it to overworked and under-appreciated translators and interpreters to create these words?

In their pride on my behalf, my colleagues were not reading the newspapers and reflecting on the Afrikaans medium Ermelo school that will not admit 'English speaking' students, or national universities that insist on remaining 'Afrikaans' even though they accept government subsidies paid with taxpayers' money. They were not reflecting on how, as mother tongue speakers of nine of the eleven official languages, we are often de facto English speakers in political arguments. My colleagues had missed the avalanche of rejections that land on Minister Naledi Pandor's lap each time she mentions mother tongue instruction.

I wished that my visiting friends could eavesdrop on how my students at the University of the Free State, where I taught for close to a decade, defended their decision not to speak more Sesotho or Xitsonga, in the world of work. 'English is an international language', they say, and therefore it should remain the de facto language of law, technology and business. Any attempt to introduce more languages will lock us out of international competitiveness and ghettoise us. Yet the Japanese, Chinese and western European economies flourish and make a mockery of these unfounded South African arguments.

Our inspired language policy is in place, we can defend it with our non-payment for services that insult us. When is corporate South Africa going to 'get with the programme'? Forget that it was in a state of denial so deep that it refused to show up at the Truth and Reconciliation Commission, what oppressive legacy is it propping up now, with our permission?

Clients should not be expected to be grateful that one of our banking institutions tokenistically offers services in isiXhosa and seSotho, among others. The corporations should speak to us in our languages, not the other way round. Most clients who purchase medicines, cereal or other products are not only English speaking. And, in a country that says our languages matter, corporate South Africa needs to move out of the apartheid dual language policy. SAA can take the lead because every time I step into one of their planes, I am sure I have travelled back in time as I gag on the offensive dual language policy.

And before we are told about how expensive it will be to translate packaging and medicine inserts, remember SABC TV and Translate.org. Nobody is so stupid as to think that translating a few paragraphs or airline greetings requires anywhere near the effort these entities have had to put into treating us with respect.

As I renew my TV license this year, I'm not paying any software license renewals for proprietary software that says I don't exist. My computer is quite happy with free software that allows me to function fully ngesiXhosa, isiZulu, Sesotho and other languages I speak.

Language matters in a variety of ways. Unfortunately, for many Black South Africans, language is also the source of deep wounding and insecurity for historical reasons. These long messy histories where pride, pleasure, wounding, shame and insecurity are deeply intertwined continue to have a very long reach into the present. The Harvard law professor and Black feminist, Patricia Williams argues that the past is not something that remains in the past. Rather, she argues, it is something that shapes every experience of the present in very specific, even if sometimes hard to discern, ways. Now, many people speak of the past's imbrications into the present, and certainly as someone whose research interest very often probes how memory and history shape collective sense of self and place, I am aware that we now take it for granted that the past is not some complete episode that we can pack away.

But I like Williams' thinking about the relationship of the past with the present as something that hovers over us like a cloud. The cloud metaphor works for Williams, not in an ominous way, but as something which sometimes casts a shadow over us as we walk beneath it. Let me stay with her conceptual metaphor for a little while. When clouds hover, they affect our experience of heat and light, so one minute we are entirely in the shade and the next we are back in the sunlight. But the cloud never goes away entirely.

Language is one of the few times where it is possible to deal directly with an aspect of historical and ongoing wounding in ways that are freeing. Part of what Simphiwe's vision suggests is the opening up of a conversation that enables us to own our languages without necessarily being yoked to ethnic nationalism.

Just as we need to develop the emotional and political vocabulary to demand that our children be taught African languages at first language level, and that corporate communicate with us in languages of our choosing, we also desperately need to uncover means of languaging our lives in ways that neither romanticise African pasts and essence, nor trap us into debilitating anxieties about ethnic nationalism. This is Simphiwe's invitation when she says 'We need to look at the past only as a reference point; we are not the people of that past. We are today's people.'

CHAPTER 6

Uncontained:

Simphiwe's Africa

The trouble is that once you see it, you can't unsee it. And once you've seen it, keeping quiet, saying nothing, becomes as political an act as speaking out. There's no innocence. Either way, you're accountable.

Arundhati Roy

Stand for the fire in your heart
Stand for the fruits of your living
Stand
Stand
Stand

Simphiwe Dana 'State of Emergency'

The uncontained Africa that Simphiwe desires is not just clear from her musical choices and lyrics. It is also apparent in her critical stance to power that finds increasing expression in her public writing and other engagements. We see evidence of what this African future resembles in her standpoints on Marikana, on the 1in9 Campaign, the tenors of institutional racism in South Africa's Western Cape Province and her altercation with Premier Helen Zille, how she languages her music and her life, who she listens to and uses as reference points in her own musical life, as well as in how she chooses to engage race, gender, pleasure, class and sexual orientation.

'Marikana' refers to the 2012 catastrophe at the Lonmin-controlled Marikana Platinum mine, near Rustenburg in the North West Province. On 10 August 2012, rock drillers went on strike for a pay rise from the R2500 they earned at the time, to R12500 a month. The strikers were not affiliated with the National Union of Mineworkers (NUM), part of the African National Congress (ANC) aligned Congress of South African Trade Unions (COSATU). Instead, the workers were members of NUM's newer competitor Association of Mineworkers and Construction Union (AMCU). The 3000 AMCU workers downed their tools after management had refused to speak to them. Two miners were killed the following day, with a further nine people comprising of two police officers, striking miners, and two security guards over the next two days. In the meantime, the miners had started to gather on various hills in the area. On 16 August, an elite police unit opened fire on strikers. Thirty-four people were killed and seventy-eight wounded in what was widely regarded as excessive use of police force. It was also the biggest use of force in post-apartheid South Africa, with several commentators making references to the Sharpeville massacre of 1960. There were conflicting police, eyewitness and journalist reports about the exact chronology of events. Police Commissioner Mangwashi Victoria Phiyega defended the police action, stating that it was a last resort by the police, after crowd control and other defensive strategies had failed, and that the police were also under attack from the miners who had clubs and machetes. Several journalists at the scene also spoke of a miner shooting at the police prior to police retaliation.

At the time of writing this, two books have come out: *Marikana: A view from the Mountain and a case to answer* by Peter Alexander,

Thapelo Lekgowa, Botsang Mmope, Luke Sinwell and Bongani Xezwi, published by Jacana Media and *Marikana: A moment in time*, a collection of essays, poems and photo essays, edited by Raphael d'Abdon and published by Gecko. The official inquiry by the Farlam Commission continues, with the evidence presented thus far re-staging the polarities evident in August. However, some of the issues that were surfaced by the event, called a tragedy by President Zuma and a massacre by many in civil society, are at the heart of power and complicity in contemporary South Africa.

The 1in9 Campaign is a feminist formation that was founded by feminists to provide support to the woman, called Khwezi, since a rape survivor may not be named, who laid a charge of rape against then Deputy President Jacob Zuma in 2005. Since then, the campaign has supported other complainants in sexual violence cases, with an organisational commitment to the realisation of sexual right. 1in9 work is activist and advocacy centred, with a vision of contributing to rebuilding a feminist movement, including queer feminism, in South Africa. Furthermore:

> While the campaign often uses cases direct interpersonal violence – particularly sexual violence – as the entry point for its activism and advocacy, it places this violence within a broader context of structural violence and historical and on-going institutionalisation of discrimination and inequality. An acknowledgement of and response to socioeconomic and political factors that underlie and maintain inequity are, therefore, built into all actions and analyses of the Campaign.

Having undergone slight change in its structure, 1in9 now focuses on five core programmes:

> [D]irect action and advocacy on specific rape cases and other issues concerning LGBT and women's rights; building solidarity with individual rape survivors and other organisations as a way to develop cross-sectoral dialogue and

collaboration; feminist media production (AMP Studio) that responds quickly to existing and emerging rights concerns and social crises; political education; knowledge creation, and feminist research, which seek to generate and give voice to grassroots feminist analyses and action; and multi-level advocacy for justice and legal transformation through direct engagement with other organisations and collectives and by influencing public discourse.

Simphiwe wrote a few poems that she dedicated to 1in9 and expressed support of some of the campaign's direct action at the 2013 Joburg Pride, where 1in9 activists had disrupted the event noting that there was little to celebrate and demanding a moment of silence for Black lesbians killed for that identity. 1in9 had a larger problem with the overall hijacking and depoliticisation of Pride from its initial founding by predominantly Black activist queers, such as Bev Ditsie and Simon Nkoli, and others to a now privately registered public party. 1in9 activists were not the only ones to take issue with the change in direction of Joburg Pride. Jabu Pereira, queer activist and co-founder of Iranti.org, a queer feminist media outfit in Johannesburg, had challenged the new organisers to answer the questions: 'How do you decide to underhandedly register a collectively owned political space as a private event?' Such a question is at the root of much of the tensions within the LGBTI community about the place of Joburg Pride, whether people feel that there needs to be renegotiation of the terms of ownership and physical delineation of space at Pride, a reclamation or boycotting of the current Pride, or other routes. The current organisers of Pride responded violently (through beating, pushing to the ground, threatening to drive over) to 1in9 activist calls to observe a moment of silence, claiming that they had misconstrued them to be homophobic protestors to the event.

Although she had initially attended Joburg Pride, upon realising the terms of contestation and what many Black queers were calling deliberate erasure, Simphiwe publicly expressed support for the position adopted by 1in9 and other Black queers against the Pride

Board. She had been equally vocal in relation to Marikana. I return to her op-ed on Marikana below.

Simphiwe will not be silenced or limited. Her Africa will not be bounded. Her consistent stance on a freer way to be African is evident across different axes of power: sexuality, sexual orientations, the right to speak, class, race and gender expression. Her responses to very different stimuli demonstrate her approach to power and commitment to justice through using her voice and visibility in support of a cause or community. It is more than a deliberate bias towards the underdog; it is a commitment to fairness and justice, and contributing to the kind of critical thinking that forms part of changing the world. It is also a refusal to be complicit and a willingness to risk being misunderstood.

Many who comment on her work continue to call her a 'Xhosa artist' and this is both true and inaccurate. She was raised by people who are Xhosa in both the language they speak and many historically informed ways of being in the world. She speaks the most distilled, elegant isiXhosa and uses this register in her songs. And she is a strong proponent of mother tongue instruction at school as much as she also advocates for African languages to be offered at first language level across the country. In the *New African Woman* interview cited earlier, Peter notes that Simphiwe is 'authentic', that her voice and music are 'pure'. The writer makes the argument that Simphiwe represents something that young Africans can emulate because of her pride in her 'Xhosa heritage'. For Peter, Simphiwe's music has abundant evidence of this pride, and the fact that Simphiwe does not shy away from discussions of her humble rural beginnings.

While I agree that Simphiwe embraces her past and location, I am not convinced that this is necessarily evidence of 'Xhosa pride'. Simphiwe is very rooted in being African and thinks that ignorance about each other lies at the heart of the xenophobic attacks in 2008 in South African urban centres. This outbreak saw many African nationals but who do not 'look' South African – often a code for darker-skinned than the range considered likely to be South African – displaced, killed and hounded out of work and home. Many testimonies also pointed to the expectation that 'real' South Africans would have access to a certain Zulu vocabulary and could be relied upon to utter the word for 'elbow' in order to pass the test by a group of men. The myth of a fairer South African population that generally speaks isiZulu well enough to know 'indololwane' saw some South Africans mistaken for 'foreigners'. Many were also known to be citizens of other countries and hounded out of communities regardless of their fluency in isiZulu and their hues. Johannesburg resident Mozambican citizen Ernesto Alfabeto Nhamuave was burnt alive by various Alexandra township residents, close to Sandton in Johannesburg, who sang anti-apartheid songs and chants and some of whom toyi-toyied as he burnt to death. Many others were displaced, sought refuge in tents, halls and police stations for the weeks that followed violence directed against them by those they had lived and worked among for varying lengths of time. Explanations of the outbreak recognised that there was a general 'xenophobic' character in many South African locations, that a competition for resources very often translated into 'foreigners' being seen as a threat and the enemy. This was one of the explanations for why there had been no similar violent attacks on middle-class Black, African 'foreign nationals'. There were no reports of similar attacks against white working-class African foreign nationals at the time.

Although explanations proliferated, very few of these moved beyond using 'class' as an explanation for why a generalised hostility erupted in the way that it did in 2008, or why then. Very few took the intersections of place, Africanness and race in this violent outbreak seriously, and consequently, many of these explanations could not account for why such violence did not proceed along other equally available lines of intra-Black prejudices, such as ethnicity. Many generalised academic arguments about xenophobic outbreaks were also circulated verbatim from research in very different contexts with little regard to localisation.

Among the more interesting responses to this negrophobic travesty included large marches through places affected by xenophobic violence organised across varied sections of the broad

South African left, public writing, short films by independent filmmakers such as Xoliswa Sithole, Akin Omotoso, Adze Ugah, Caroline Carew, Rehad Desai, Desiree Markgraaf, Andy Spitz, Omelga Mthiyane, Riaan Hendricks, Marianne Gysae, Don Edkind, Kyle O'Donoghue, Dylan Valley, Miki Redelinghuys, Lauren Groenewald, Jyoti Mistry, Danny Turken, Khalid Shamis and Neil Brandt, who formed themselves into Filmmakers Against Racism, and used their resources to make these films which they all used to spark discussion at screenings in community venues across the country, as well as essays by various intellectuals collected into *Go Home or Die Here: Violence, xenophobia and the re-invention of difference* edited by professors Shireen Hassim, Tawana Kupe and Eric Worby, and published by Wits University Press in 2008. Simphiwe is also not interested in ethnic nationalism, or, to use the colonial formulation that many people insist on using, 'tribal' affiliation. Indeed, Simphiwe has often argued that if people from South Africa travelled more on the continent, physically and imaginatively, as she tells Peter:

we would have so much love and respect for the rest of the African people. We have self-hate as African people. We should not be embarrassed by our poverty, this is not of our own doing, and we should not accept hand-outs but be given a proper chance to also make it. I know there are some who have been given that chance and have used it effectively to build themselves.

Simphiwe is not an ethnic nationalist. She is deeply in love with exploring what it means to be African. She speaks isiZulu, has made a conscious effort to learn to speak, read and write seTswana, talks about learning kiSwahili and several other languages. She also wishes – not so secretly – that there was a shared African language that we all spoke on the continent. Many of her songs are rendered in isiXhosa which ranges from a beautiful, most pristine refined idiom to sensual and playful to a 'little black girl's idiom' that I battle to name in English, or even explain adequately in the other languages that I speak. Being a polyglot and wordsmith sometimes means we have to craft the language to name what we mean. Some people have called it '*ishori*' and we see it in how she speaks about carrying that purse she has even when it is empty as she walks down Bantu Biko Street. Here '*ishori*' sits side to side with the very serious political aesthetic of the song. Her song '*Ndiredi*' presents one of the ways we see something about her approach to language. She is not a language purist in an ethnic nationalist sense. In fact, she clearly has no loyalty to ethnic chauvinism. Simphiwe identifies as African not just in what she says, but who she listens to repeatedly in her house, the books she carries, buys, reads and shares. She is a global citizen, but she is very African by association and choice. Her excitement and joy when listening to Nigerian singer Asa belies how much of Asa's music she plays. And when she reads Nigerian novelist Ben Okri, whom she really loves, you can see her restraining herself from reading every word on the page aloud. It does not even matter if she knows you have read the book.

The professor of literature and cultural theorist, James Ogude says 'Africa is in the range of templates', and this captures some of how Simphiwe relates to things African. For Ogude, there is no one Africa that is secure and 'authentic'. There are African forms of play, humour, prayer or discipline. We can often find African texture, inflection or spirit. However, to fix things and police others in search of the 'African' is neither interesting nor worthwhile. At least, this is some of what Ogude means. Simphiwe is interested in seeing which templates work, and work for her, when. What can we mix and match? What can we remix? What is frightening? At her best, she is highly questioning of herself. Hers is a consistently unapologetic stance on African location and identity without shying away from difficulty. Simphiwe speaks from a place that she is constantly crafting, changing, reshaping. She also uses her visibility in the interest of expanding this.

At the end of Zukiswa Wanner's 'Simphiwe: South Africa's emerging force', published in *Africa Review* in April 2011, the editor saw fit to insert the following comment:

Simphiwe Dana is a great performer who seems to be going for Miriam Makeba's shoes but her music distributors and manager need to do a better job if the rest of Africa matters to them.

Wanner writes in the piece how the same editor had initially been lukewarm when Wanner had pitched the idea of a piece on her, until he was so mesmerised by Simphiwe's performance at the 12ᵗʰ Cape Town International Jazz Festival in 2011.

This uncontained Africa of Simphiwe's grasping is everywhere evident not just in her music and her taste, but in her engagement with pressing South African concerns too. Interviewing Simphiwe on her increasingly vocal presence on various South African issues, journalist Percy Zvomuya writes in 'Simphiwe Dana unplugged', published in *Mail and Guardian* on 10 February 2012:

Those who follow Dana on Twitter – about 24 000 – will know of her tenacious and at times aggressive approach to dialogue when she senses an injustice. She says her social-activism persona came to the surface during the time she spent in the city. '[It] pushed me to confront certain things. The activism was inspired by Cape Town.'

Late last year Dana got into a Twitter spat with the premier of the Western Cape, Helen Zille, who is also the leader of the Democratic Alliance, in a contribution to the topic 'Cape Town is racist'. The debate – more like an electronic brawl – started when a Twitter user, Lindiwe Suttle, wrote: 'No matter how famous/rich you are, you're still a 2nd class citizen if you're black in Cape Town' – a statement Zille dismissed as 'complete nonsense' and 'a baseless assertion'.

The Twitter battle, covered word for word in *The Times*, escalated when Dana responded: 'Are you disputing that it's racist?' She added: 'It's embarrassing that as a leader you would deny people their experiences. Try live in a black skin for once. You have the power to change things. Use it!' Zille retorted: 'You're a highly respected black professional.

Don't try to be a professional black. It demeans you.'

The debate descended into a bare-knuckled free-for-all that was never quite resolved. The two were then invited to take part in a radio programme and, as is the nature of these spats, neither of them backed down.

Dana says: 'Ma Zille put her [foot] in it. She did start it.' She adds: 'I was really offended. I am still waiting for my apology.' Yet she is keen to state that this episode does not signal her entry into politics. In fact, she is adamant that what she does is not politics, preferring instead to call it 'social activism'. She says: 'I have no political ambitions. Zille doesn't have to worry. I'm not trying to get her job.'

Zvomuya aptly captures both the episode and Dana's own stance both on Twitter as well as in her op-eds on Capetonian racism. In an earlier interview, published in the same paper on 19 September 2010, under the title 'My City: Cape Town', when asked by Ziphezinhle Msimango 'What's the ugliest thing about Cape Town?' Simphiwe answered:

As I am black, I cannot deny the racism. It's in the air. It's entrenched in the psyche of the white people, and the black people of Cape Town have internalised it to a point that they are apologetic about being black. Yes, I said it.

What followed was a demonstration of the ways in which many South Africas exist but not all of them can or dare be spoken. This is something that is also clear in Simphiwe's attempt to contribute to education through her Black Culture Education Tour and *stokvels*, as well as in her public writing on the state of South Africa. Public responses tell us something about how certain eruptions are not stand-alone but part of a larger tapestry. The Black Culture Education Tour and *stokvels* were Simphiwe's attempt to raise funds through her own performances (in the case of the former) and in collaboration with like-minded people and collectives, in order to intervene into the public education crisis in post-apartheid South Africa. In this chapter I read Simphiwe's activist moments not as isolated, but as part of using her prominence and voice to question existing inequality. Her public commentary and disagreements are met with much enthusiasm, some receptive and some defensive. She seems to be grappling with much that the anti-racist and public gender discourses in South Africa miss. In many instances, she is met with correction that attempts to contain her views or silence her altogether. You are a musician not a politician, they insist. Why don't you stick to your place as a woman, instead of questioning things that don't concern you, they push back. Why would you want to be 'that kind' of Black person when it would be easier to be the kind that makes me more comfortable, they tweet.

But Simphiwe is not content to sit quietly, feeling victimised by sometimes quite extensive harassment by those who feel called to defend the subjects of her criticisms. She is as unwavering in her desire to live outside correction as she is in her commitment to graft a new register to imagine and speak. She speaks from a place that she is constantly crafting, changing, reshaping; and is unwavering in using her visibility to cast more spotlight on what she sees as neglected. This requires taking risks, and because she is human she does sometimes get it very wrong. For example, when she is particularly incensed about a particular injustice, especially if it is being played out in a part of the world beyond South Africa's borders, she will often punctuate her critique or statement of solidarity with a statement that suggests that everybody else has turned a blind eye to what she decries. Examples of this include:

Afrikans were massacred by anti Gaddafi forces post his assassination. We didn't bat an eyelid.

The killing of innocent children in Gaza by apartheid Israel breaks my heart. And the world is hardly moved.

We are yet to interrogate the psychology of our oppression. Until then... things fall apart.

The problem with this is that at any given point, there are people working very hard to address the very same issue, sometimes an extremely active and highly visible globally and in South Africa, pro-Palestinian movement. The third statement is particularly odd since it erases her own project. And Steve Biko's. And various African feminists' and queer activists'. All of these are people she works and stands in solidarity with. At times, these activists are laying their lives on the line. Although well-intentioned, such punctuation does not recognise these efforts or privileges the behaviours of states over activists who do lead to the shifts we see in policy and conflict. While these instances by Simphiwe are often quick statements on social media, given that I have chosen to treat her public utterances on all media as important, it would be disingenuous to leave these uncommented on.

Speaking at a National Social Cohesion Summit in Kliptown, in Soweto, on 4 July 2012, the leader of the South African parliamentary opposition, the Democratic Alliance, and Western Cape Premier Helen Zille was excited by the possibility of a socially cohesive society where active citizenship was the norm. She defined this situation along the following lines:

> It means citizens who care about using their opportunities in life, and who take responsibility for using them, because every citizen is an active partner in his or her own development and that of the country. Opportunity only makes a difference if you use it. And there can be no nation-building without active, responsible citizens using their opportunities for the benefit of the country.

In the same speech, Zille noted that what her political party, the Democratic Alliance, has learnt is that 'there are no short-cuts to social cohesion', where social cohesion is really 'about people living together harmoniously, feeling a sense of belonging, and participating in the civic and social life of their communities'. She continued to define social cohesion as that which 'also means balancing rights with responsibilities. Individuals, communities, and governments must all take responsibility'.

I have no doubt that Zille espouses these values; she also claims them as the vision that shapes her political party. This is what the DA often refers to as an equal opportunity society. At the same time, every political formation has variance within, so to claim a party vision often articulates an ideal rather than describing a reality. Zille's statement above underscores the difficult work required in order to achieve the goal of social cohesion achievable through active citizenship and a sense of responsibility among the public. Zille's own biography shows evidence of how she subscribes to these values, whether one looks at her former journalistic career or her rise to her current position as one of the most influential leaders in a political terrain that is explicitly masculinist and hostile to women.

Simphiwe seems to have taken these professed ideals and recognitions at face value. She was not responding to Zille's comments at the Kliptown venue. However, what Zille said in the speech from which I have drawn excerpts (the full text is available on the DA's website, as are the other comments directly attributed to senior women in the party) is consistent with what she has said elsewhere. She places value on responsible, active citizenship, freedom of expression, the exercise of responsibility, the use of privilege and access to widen justice, and the centrality of the democratic use of ordinary citizen's voices to hold government accountable. All of these are important in order to build this apparently desired future state where we can have a more cohesive state. Interestingly, as listed here, Simphiwe can be said to subscribe to the exact same values. Such a list suggests that Ms Dana and Premier Zille are much closer in their values regarding public political life than exchanges between them show.

Furthermore, as another senior politician points out, this time the party's Parliamentary Leader, Lindiwe Mazibuko, the DA takes access to leaders seriously. The DA's social media activity directly supports this claim. This approach is not divorced from the high usage of e-tools and the visibility of DA office holders within the organisation as well as in public office and on social media. Unlike other political parties within South Africa that seem to view online presence as superfluous, the DA considers it a crucial part of how the party interfaces with various publics. When we consider the accessibility of mobile telephony, and the overlap between the overwhelmingly young social media users and young voting population in South Africa, the wisdom in the DA's media strategy is obvious. In a speech to the Global Media Forum 2012 delivered in Bonn, Germany, on 26 June 2012, Mazibuko argued that her political party's approach to new media was part of bringing about permanent change to the South African political scene. The party is aware of the implications of itself being 'wired, connected and networked' while the ruling party, the African National Congress depended largely 'on old fashioned mediums to communicate their message and remain stuck in the 1980s trade union style campaigning'. Mazibuko continued:

I have the privilege of leading the official opposition in the National Assembly. In contrast to my counterparts in the ANC, I am proud to say I remain 'connected' the entire time both inside and outside of parliament. In South Africa, the DA is seeking to pioneer a new kind of activist politics in which everyone can participate from the city dweller to the remotest villager.

Due to South Africa's vast geographical territory, the new technologies mean that my DA colleagues and I can constantly interact with the public. The DA is the most digitally savvy political party in South Africa, and this reflects the dynamism and creativity of our fast-changing society.

Our social media campaign is always positive, and enables us to speak to people in a way that is not mediated by the traditional press. One could call it the new politics of the neighbourhood.

This is especially the case and apt in a country where 95 per cent of people have access to cellular phones, and more than 70 per cent to the internet, where 14 per cent of people had access to internet on their desktops, and 10 per cent of the population use Facebook, she pointed out. In this country, Premier Zille has more Twitter followers that President Zuma, where most people on social media are in the 18–34 range and therefore presumed to be the future power base. Interestingly, she also asserts that 'the DA also uses Twitter to find new talent and ideas', further illustrating both the innovation and the 'equal opportunity' approaches claimed by the organisation.

The exchanges between Helen Zille and Simphiwe Dana demonstrate the ways in which claiming adherence to the same values does not necessarily translate into mutual recognition and intelligibility. Even though the DA and ANC are diametrically opposed in terms of the positions within the South African political landscape, there are similarities in how they deal with critical engagement from outside their ranks. Zille's exchange with Simphiwe as well as her interpretations of the angry racialised responses to some of her tweets suggests that she misreads the position from which her detractors speak.

In spite of all these claims to access and a willingness to engage, however, it is very clear that how Helen Zille reads the speaking position of those she converses with on Twitter directly shapes what she publicly entertains. This can be read as a paradox given the values stated above, or, less generously as Zille's unwillingness to engage those who do not start from the premise of agreeing to the DA's paradigms. It is possible to read her as projecting duality onto those she disagrees with. Here, then, she assumes that all people who are incensed by her specific use of racially loaded language are ANC members or sympathisers, as is clear in her responses to being taken on for using the imagery of 'refugees' and 'professional black' on Twitter in 2012, in relation to Simphiwe Dana and migrants from the Eastern Cape to the Western Cape province.

On 8 April 2012, writing in her online missive 'Personal reflections on three weeks of outrage', she discusses the unwillingness of people to step out of their contained categories.

She writes:

> Some readers may recall the commotion that ensued when it was alleged that I had called singer Simphiwe Dana a 'professional black'. Actually, that is precisely the opposite of what I said. I called her a 'highly respected black professional'. No matter how many times I pointed out the difference, the false perception was reinforced by repetition.

On this score, Premier Zille misses the cause of the outrage. There are two ways to read the tweet. In Zille's reading, she did not accuse Simphiwe of being a 'professional Black'. Therefore there is no cause for anger. Indeed, Zille, to be fair, pointed out that Simphiwe was not a professional Black, but a Black professional. Zille's point was that Dana's mode of disagreement with her demonstrated aspects of 'professional Black' behaviour. And she did clarify this several times on Twitter. In the angry twiteratti's reading, it is the category 'professional Black' that is angering, not its proximity or non-proximity, to Simphiwe Dana. In other words, the reason for all of these clarifications from Zille is because they were not addressing the cause of the anger. The clarifications were ineffective in mediating (or modulating) the anger because Zille and her detractors were speaking past each other, with increasing levels of frustration on both sides. Black Twitter was not simply defending Simphiwe from imagined harm. The fact of the matter is that the rage was caused, 'clarifications' notwithstanding. The misunderstanding of what she said was *minimal* in causing offense. The rage coalesced around two things that Zille could not recognise. Simphiwe's involvement was important to both, but they were also not *just* about Simphiwe.

First, the problem is with the very category 'professional Black' that many found offensive. A professional Black is someone who insists that race continues to matter in more ways than the DA claims. A professional Black may be sympathetic to the ANC, but she may have as little time for the ANC as she does for the DA. The very terminology of 'professional Black' is problematic because it pathologises, trivialises, and renders as abnormal a certain anti-racist stance that Zille does not embrace. Neither the ANC nor the DA seems attentive to some of the emerging ways in which critical race consciousness articulates for contemporary South African social media communities. South African Twitter is highly racialised, even if some of the ways in which this racialisation is articulated do not neatly fit into ways readily recognisable through ANC and/or DA rhetoric. Zille's appellation 'professional Black' was translated variously into the equivalent of 'Blacks with a chip on their shoulder' and 'uppity Blacks', with those exact phrases cropping up with remarkable frequency during the episode. It is the equivalent of the dismissal of blacks who have a 'chip on their shoulder' for seeing racism and naming it as such in order to silence. Therefore, when Zille said someone was *not* a 'professional Black' or telling her to stop acting like the category 'professional Black', she insists that this was not a racial insult. Those who fought with her on Twitter disagreed. There may have been no direct insult to Simphiwe, they argued, but you are in fact doing so to whoever occupies the category you name 'professional Blacks'. In other words, saying 'don't be that kind of person/ you are not that kind of person' is just saying that the 'kind of person' under discussion is beneath the one you addressed. Given the fact that many of the respondents on Black Twitter see themselves as exhibiting a similar stance to what white supremacy has historically called 'uppity negroes/Blacks', Zille may not have disapproved of Simphiwe, but she clearly disapproved of them. In other words, the anger was in their own defence. In the language of this logic, Zille's formulation threw 'professional Blacks' under the bus.

The second problem pertains to the mode of address that comes with telling people how to behave appropriately. Telling Simphiwe that she should steer clear of acting like a 'professional Black' because another category, 'Black professional' is more appropriate is policing what is appropriate and silencing the critique. This is akin to deciding on 'dangerous' (uppity) Blacks versus 'good' Blacks. It is not for her to decide.

Helen Zille's insistence that she had borrowed this term not from white supremacist language but from a Black intellectual, in this case Jacob Dlamini, did nothing to assuage the anger. But Zille's statement is important in clarifying why this incident puzzled her. Part of what she was, in fact, signalling was how seriously she does take ideas in the public domain. Dlamini's phrase had allowed her to articulate something specific. She assumes she could be heard in the same ways Dlamini could be because she is invested in an equal opportunity society, and for her, its creation is partly through proceeding as though it already exists. In other words, you create an equal opportunity society by acting as though it exists. Its performance is its creation.

However, for Simphiwe and the many who were angered by Zille, an equitable society is created differently. What constitutes its creation (enacting it until it becomes) for Zille, is itself a performance of denial for her detractors. Some of the frustration also stems from the fact that this loosely formed group does take Zille seriously as a politician. They also hold her to a high standard, one that recognises that she has to negotiate constant correction and inappropriate gendered public commentary. The irony is that here was a serious leader who was herself in spite of routine trivialisation through a running commentary on her attire, body size, alleged cosmetic choices, performing a similar censoring mode, this time around Blackness.

But this is not really ironic, for to be subjected to patriarchal control and censure does not automatically discourage you from enacting the same along a different power axis. Otherwise Black men could not be patriarchal, Black heterosexual women could not be homophobic and middle-class white women could not be oppressive to poor women.

It may not stop women in the public from acting in ways that are consistent with their political choices, but patriarchal violence and policing are still harmful. But even transgressive, critical political actors, are still plagued by the same human contradictions that I discussed in an earlier chapter, according to one reading. If Premier Zille in fact acts in gender terms as though she does live in an equal opportunity society, then in her reading of the exchange, there is consistency. The problem is that neither side can consider a world in which both readings can be valid at the same time.

She does not understand that people can *both* be outraged by the ANC's irresponsibility and institutional violence against children through the education system, and be angered by her use of language that was used to render Black South Africans illegitimate at the same time. Yet, this is exactly what is at play here. However, because she does not want to take responsibility for her recent, repeated public reversion to using offensive race language, she refers to any attempts to hold her accountable 'pseudo outrage'.

It does not matter which Black South Africans she calls 'refugees'. There is never an instance where this does not resemble too closely the apartheid logic of homelands and townships as the places where Black people belong, while 'South Africa' was a place they needed passports and permits to occupy. The fact that she added 'education' to 'refugee' does not change anything. In a democracy, it is not necessary to criminalise movements in order to criticise the causes of that migration. Yet this is what Zille does. In her commitment to criticising the deplorable conditions of education under the ANC government, she considers the harm in naming the 'victim' collateral damage. The outrage stems from the fact that those she would call 'professional blacks' find the latter stance unacceptable.

In 'Twitter storm is clouding the real issue', published online on 28 March 2012, Zille further resorts to showing why 'refugee' should not be offensive. First, she says this is because her own family were once refugees. Therefore she would not use the appellation 'refugee' in insulting ways. In other words, she claims insider use of the language. She writes:

There is absolutely nothing pejorative or racist in the word 'refugee'. Indeed it is actually intended to be an affirmation of people and an indictment of the authorities that denied and trampled on their rights in the first place.

My parents were refugees (in the United Nations' narrow definition of the word). Perhaps because I grew up in a refugee family, I don't find the term insulting at all. For me, it evokes empathy for the struggle that people face in re-establishing their lives in a new place.

Like most other refugees, my parents started out poor, and worked extremely hard to provide their children the opportunities they never had. My father began his working life as a manual labourer, and advanced to delivering bread, while studying at night. Eventually he started a small business. I never once heard him complain about his lot in life. My parents taught us to take responsibility and never to perceive ourselves as victims. Only as an adult can I sufficiently appreciate their guidance and wisdom. Much of this, I believe in retrospect, grew out of the fact that they were refugees. They were strong, principled, and never blamed their plight on others. They certainly weren't 'professional offence takers' or 'insult seekers'.

Personally, I was not compelled to move to the Western Cape from Gauteng to secure my basic rights. I came because I had fallen in love and wanted to follow my heart. So I suppose I could be called a 'romantic refugee', one of a growing number world-wide. Whatever, I don't consider the term an insult, in any form.

The problem with this is that the family members she describes really *were* accurately refugees. Nobody is pretending that real refugees do not exist in the world, or even in South Africa. Against this backdrop, to say there are refugees in her family history sidesteps the issue.

She then writes:

Let me start by saying that a refugee, in its broad definition, is 'someone who seeks refuge' because their rights are denied or suppressed where they live. There are different refugee categories. The United Nations defines a refugee as someone who seeks refuge across a national border (because that has implications for UN funding and other interventions). People who are forced to relocate within the borders of their own country because their rights are abused or denied are called 'Internally Displaced Persons.' They are a refugee category – and their refugee status is becoming increasingly recognised internationally.

In other words, what Zille is arguing in the above paragraph is that the reason people should not take offence is because they are refugees in a technical sense, since people who are displaced within the borders of their countries are also called 'refugees' as far as the UN is concerned. It is a technical point that covers her own use of the term that offends. Therefore the ones who take issue with her usage of 'education refugee' are looking for excuses to feign anger because she has used accurate language, technically.

However, Zille is being disingenuous here. According to the 1951 Refugee Convention wording that established the United Nations High Commission for Refugees, a refugee is a person who

> owing to a well-founded fear of being persecuted for reasons of race, religion, nationality, membership of a particular social group or political opinion, *is outside the country of his nationality*, and is unable to, or owing to such fear, is unwilling to avail himself of the protection of that country.

I have added the emphasis. Technically, Zille is incorrect. You are only a refugee if you are forced to leave your country due to a range of reasons because you cannot enjoy the protection of your home country. The Western Cape is not a country separate from South Africa. The people about whom Zille speaks clearly *do* enjoy the protection of their country through *her* and her party's governance of a province within their country. In case there is still confusion – which clearly there is, and not just in Zille's conception – on its own website, the contents of which are copyrighted until 2012, the UNHCR writes that it also helps a category labelled 'Internally Displaced People'. It proceeds to note:

Internally displaced people, or IDPs, are often wrongly called refugees. Unlike refugees, IDPs have not crossed an international border to find sanctuary but have remained inside their home countries. Even if they have fled for similar reasons as refugees (armed conflict, generalized violence, human rights violations), IDPs legally remain under the protection of their own government – even though that government might be the cause of their flight. As citizens, they retain all of their rights and protection under both human rights and international humanitarian law.

For the UNHCR, the distinctions are clear – technically and legally – and distinguishing is important. Why would Zille then simply make this up? She could have just used the technically correct terminology but she did not. Instead, she used language which sounded very close to apartheid legislation that said Black people could not legitimately move around in South Africa because it was not their country. She *could* have just said 'I meant Internally Displaced People. I was misinformed about IDPs as a type of refugee in a technical sense'. Instead, she performed increasingly bizarre self-defences which are a refusal to take responsibility for harm inflicted, even if unintentionally.

Much more perversely, Zille insists on 'being right' in relation to how race continues to matter (*only* in the narrow ways that are convenient for her and the DA), in relation to what people may legitimately be angered by, and her refusal to recognise that active citizenship can – and is – exercised though the questioning of both the ANC and the DA in many instances.

I used to think that the DA was a liability to her leadership, that she possibly had more vision than her conservative party that claims 'liberal' values. Her responses to critique by private citizens in exactly the same way that she responds to the ANC shows that this is not the case; she may be a liability to her party, even with the limited growth we see in its numbers. Her refusal to act like a liberal in the classic definition, to take responsibility for damage she inflicts, to recognise the real ways in which race continues to matter and how these meanings differ for different ideologically located groups, and take seriously views that radically differ from her own rather than dismiss them *precisely* because they are not her own or from those she considers safe, are at the core of why the DA is not a viable party for the large – and growing – numbers of Black South Africans who are disillusioned and disappointed with how the ANC rules. Simphiwe once tweeted something that is in line with this statement thus:

> The ANC has hurt a lot of us. But I'd rather eat my vote than give it to neo-colonialist DA.

This is a new time at the level of collective consciousness in South Africa. She has tweeted that she fears 'South Africa will not survive Zuma'. Many others for whom democracy became increasingly complicated after the end of a brutal colonial regime have been here before us. We can learn from that, or choose not to. Choosing the former requires that we spend time looking both inward and elsewhere. Gabeba Baderoon speaks about something similar when she says:

> This is a particular moment that has allowed us to inhabit the spaces of our humanity more fully, I think. Some people whom I encounter overseas find me a little outside the arena they know as South African poetry. In South Africa I never find that. Here, we have actually entered a time when the political is known to include the full humanity of people, so that in addition to resistance, we can explore our madness and failures and doubts and loves. And at the same time, to draw a solid line under apartheid is deluded and dangerous.

This moment has implications for the imagination, and what to do with uncertainty. It also has to do with being disappointed by many aspects of our democracy. Simphiwe has a new single 'State of Emergency' (2012), released through various electronic channels that speaks to these concerns.

In 'State of Emergency' from her forthcoming album, Simphiwe's voice is in rare appearance in English musically. Yet it is nonetheless recognisably hers in the haunting melody and voice that looks back in as much as it is a call to conscience and action. It is also the English that best captures what she talks about, what she achieves aesthetically and rhetorically in this song. The footage in the 'international version' of the video with subtitles, juxtaposes iconic imagery and press coverage. Older South African audiences will recognise young people carrying coffins at political funerals, the figure of anti-apartheid leader Alan Boesak, burnt carcasses of cars, militarised township youth with eyes wide open in defiance and the survival as various figures walk streets strewn with tyres, rocks and cans in the immediate aftermath of a street uprising. There is smoke rising from cars and buildings with groups of apartheid police officers in the streets.

Interlocked with this very powerful visual language, of memory, association and emotional evocation, Simphiwe's backgrounded voice sings of youth leaving crying parents as they took charge of the political sphere. As Dana's voice sings of brutality and defiance, as well as of the names of the horrid leaders of apartheid 'trending in the streets', she is speaking of both the importance of keeping memory alive and speaking in the language of today's youth: the language of the Twitter generation where the most discussed issues 'trend' on 'Twitter streets'.

It is an apt metaphor and, as she uses the powerfully ambiguous language of 'state sponsored Black on Black violence', is she speaking of the past or the present? The call to stand, repeated several times in the chorus, is both a description of the past and an invitation to stand. In this song, Simphiwe calls for us to stand up, to stop sitting or taking things lying down, to stand for something. She reminds us that in the past people conjured up the courage to get us where we are: freer, but not quite free. *They* stood.

Where is today's youth, she asks alongside the question mark of where the youth of the iconic Soweto uprisings in 1976 is. She obviously does not mean that they need to take charge of the country again. Some are in charge of the country today as it is, and we have the disastrous manner in which the Lonmin miners' strike in Marikana was handled, such that many dubbed the police response a massacre against the state's labelling of the bloodbath as a tragedy; the youth of 1976 presides over a collapsed education system and a floundering health system. But Simphiwe is also asking about the power and spirit of courage that permeated that time, about the legacy of courage and resolve in today's youth. She is asking a question in the spirit of the song by Thandiswa Mazwai I analysed in 'Desiring Simphiwe: the soft feminist'.

She is careful not to glorify heroism, though, because she repeats how hard it was in the hauntingly resung 'they take everything to God' and 'prayer and wailing in Soweto'. The 'sell-out Black leaders' she mentions are both some of the youth of 1976 and the ones that the youth of 1976, and their successor, should confront. Instead, we have the paradox: 'forgotten memories festering in the youth'. Here, Simphiwe points to both the contradictions and the ironies of a democracy in which so many young people have no hope of jobs whether they go to school or not. They are therefore trapped in poverty. This reality of present-day SA tells our youth that 'the revolution has fallen'.

Literature professor and award-winning filmmaker, Bhekizizwe Peterson argues that:

One of the astounding characteristics of the 'new' South Africa has been the lack of generosity in according moments and spaces for people to deal with the complexities of mourning and healing... Post-apartheid South Africa has tended to conjoin and simplify the individual body and the body-politic as similar in their experiences of social violence and ways of recovering from its impact. Hence the expectation on the victims and survivors of apartheid atrocity, in light of the powerful arguments for forgiveness and reconciliation, is to forgo personal concerns and needs in favour of national ones. In such framing, forgiveness becomes a disempowering burden, especially if attempts to 'deal with the past' are pejoratively associated with the pursuit of not truth and justice but 'vengeance' and 'retribution'.

Simphiwe's work is partly a rejection of the narrative Peterson variously problematises in his own work, such as the brilliant film *Zulu Love Letter* that he made with Ramadan Suleman.

But it is not a new approach in Simphiwe's work. In her second album and the one which seems to have been least well-received but which she also calls her best one so far, she has the song '*Sizo Phum' eLokishini*', which speaks powerfully both to the ruling party's implication in what she would call 'State of Emergency' later, but also responds to what is at the heart of her altercation with Zille and her refusal to accept that place is always political. The song is not written to the ANC or DA, but its message is relevant long after its release as commentary on 'educational refugee', on unemployment, on the Marikana massacre.

'*Sizo Phum' eLokishini*' is about not celebrating township existence, which is a courageous stance that can be hard to follow for South Africa right now because it seems at odds with notions of locating Black life in township as 'authentic', or as ghetto-fabulous. Here, Simphiwe was saying something that may be quite jarring within the context of post-apartheid South Africa. People must have thought she was saying we are not ghetto-fabulous, and they did not know how to deal with that and the fact that the bulk of the conservative discourse in post-apartheid South Africa says that we should all move out and get affluent by going to a certain kind of suburb.

However, Simphiwe was saying something bigger and much more profound: let us not limit ourselves to the township when the whole continent could be and should be ours. She insists that there is a danger in locating Blackness in townships. This danger is of saying that we are all we were made to be. Yes, Black people created beautiful things and much pleasure even though they were put there against their will. However, for Simphiwe, part of honouring that survival and creativity is in retaining ownership of township legacies at the same time as distancing ourselves from those parts of it that are limiting and debilitating. We can do both: we can be so much more than we limit ourselves to be. She is saying something that resonates with the global Black feminist mantra: 'it's not either or; it's both and'.

My interpretation of this song is certainly supported by the song, but also by her preoccupation with expanding the imagination. We had heard it in the refrain in *'wandinikelan' amaphiko xa ungafuni ndiwasebenzise'*, (which translates into why endow me with wings I may not use?). It's also in the flying metaphors I discuss in another chapter. The insistence on being more, managing contradictions, is also vividly expressed in *'Ndiredi'*, the anthem from her debut album *Zandisile*, which is *not* her daughter's name, even though article after article continues to insist it is. The sense of flight not as running away, but as freedom, permission taken to let her spread her wings is echoed in the lyrics beyond her debut album, in how she lives her life, in her invitation to us all in this song about leaving the township.

The album *The One Love Movement on Bantu Biko Street* had BBC nominations, and excellent reviews everywhere, but sold worst and was less understood in South Africa. Simphiwe is quite frustrated by this, but I think it makes perfect sense. In an interview that Kimberley A Yates and I did with one of the founder members of the Black Consciousness Movement in South Africa, Mamphela Ramphele, which was published in the feminist journal *Agenda* in 1998, on early Black Consciousness and activism, Ramphele talks about her sadness in relation to Black Consciousness in the late 1990s. She says she is saddened that Steve Biko's intellect 'has not left a deeper imprint on the South African landscape than it could have'. Simphiwe calls for a return and re-engagement with Black Consciousness tenets.

Part of the shock and attempts to contain Simphiwe is because she speaks about things she is ostensibly not qualified to speak about. Arundhati Roy reminds us that abrogating things to those whose careers, education or placement marks them as experts, as Zille's response suggests, is *not* the way to go. In fact, for Roy, it is decisively one of the most dangerous things we can do to ourselves and the world, especially when it comes to decisions made by politicians and/or corporate entities.

In her essay, 'Shall we leave it to the experts?', she asserts that for the elite beneficiaries of any society, 'leaving it to the experts', can be beneficial. It is a

> convenient way of shrugging off your own role in the circuitry. And it creates a huge professional market for all kinds of 'expertise'. There's a whole ugly universe waiting to be explored there.

Simphiwe Dana may have felt something akin to what Roy details in the longer version of this essay, initially presented as the Third Annual Eqbal Ahmad Lecture in March 2001, at Hampshire College, Massachusetts and published in her book, *Power Politics*, in her chapter 'The Ladies have feelings, so shall we leave it to the experts?', that to witness the large scale disparity and ongoing injustice, feels like

> your face is slammed right up against it. To address it, to deal with it, to not deal with it, to try and understand it, to insist on not understanding it, to simply survive it – on a daily basis, hourly basis – is a fine art in itself. Either an art or form of insular, inward-looking insanity. Or both... To be a writer in a country where something akin to an undeclared civil war is being waged on its subjects in the name of 'development' is an onerous responsibility.

Substituting the word 'South Africa' for 'India', I turn to Roy, again from that first chapter to her book *Power Politics*, to capture what is akin to Simphiwe Dana's position on speaking about injustice, whether it is against the DA in her tussles with Helen Zille, against the government and ruling party in her essay on Marikana ('Marikana was the uprising of the poor', published on the front page of *The Sunday Independent*'s Dispatches section,

13 August 2012), her open letter to Steve Biko published on her blog, or her new song 'State of Emergency'. Roy also says:

> The fact is that what's happening in India today is not a problem, and the issues that some of us are raising are not causes. They are huge political and social upheavals that are convulsing the nation. One is not involved by virtue of being a writer or activist. One is involved because one is a human being. Writing about it just happens to be the most effective thing I can do. I think it is vital to de-professionalize the public debate on matters that vitally affect the lives of ordinary people. It's time to snatch our futures back from the 'experts'. Time to ask, in ordinary language, the public question and to demand, in ordinary language, the public answer. Frankly, however trenchantly, however angrily, however combatively one puts forward one's case, at the end of the day, I'm only a citizen, one of many, who is demanding public information, asking for a public explanation. I have no axe to grind. I have no professional stakes to protect. I am prepared to be persuaded. I'm prepared to change my mind. But instead of an argument, or an explanation, or a disputing of facts, one gets insults, invective, legal threats, and the Expert's anthem: 'You're too emotional. You don't understand, and it's too complicated to explain.' The subtext, of course, is: Don't worry your little head about it. Go and play with your toys. Leave the real world to us.

Roy says when people respond as Zille did, in fact, what is going on is

> the pitting of one value system against another, one kind of political instinct against another. It's interesting to watch so many supposedly 'rational' people turn into irrational, instinctive political beings. To see how they find reasons to support their views, and how, if those reasons are argued away, they continue to cling to their views anyway. Perhaps

for this alone, provocation is important. In a crisis, it helps clarify who's on which side.

Simphiwe will not embrace victimhood and lack of intellect. Politics needs to make sense to ordinary citizens, not just be the terrain of a specifically ordained political class. It should also be possible to speak it in the language of ordinary citizenry, not merely the professionalised discourses of the politicians and analysts. What disturbs about Simphiwe Dana is that she is neither of the convenient binaries that are bandied about by many analysts: she is clearly not DA and clearly not ANC. How she votes is irrelevant. The point is that she speaks her mind: it is very clear that like a not insignificant number of people, she is not convinced of the discourse that we are caught between two binaries.

Zille and those who defend her against Simphiwe can no more recognise where Ms Dana speaks from than can the Tripartite ruling Alliance. They all think she speaks out of turn. In a South Africa that constantly claims fatigue at some of the shenanigans of the ANC but bemoans the absence of a viable alternative, Simphiwe is a refreshing perspective that suggests that perhaps that alternative needs to be created, that attention to the past and the present are important, but an alternative that serves South Africa needs to be fashioned. This imaginative process requires the courage of risk, and perhaps because she is an artist, it is possible to speak 'out of turn' and play around with possibility, for this is what creativity is, after all.

Public discourse has to be public. Every politician publicly claims to subscribe to this principle. It is a principle that means we have to be able to access it, enter into it, not just because we are specialists. But this is not the reality. Of course, Simphiwe is not the average person, but if her participation can be so contested that Zille tries to contain and silence, rather than engage her, perhaps this casts into better light how the public sphere is not completely open to all participation, except maybe the new social media platforms.

This is also why social media platforms are so important and disruptive. Whether on these platforms or on older ones, Simphiwe Dana, like Arundhati Roy, is convinced that political and public talk must make sense to citizens, be recognisable, be theoretically accessible even if not accessed. In other words, people have to be able to recognise themselves in how they are spoken about, for and so forth and be able to speak in their own name to those in public office. This is part of how to hold public officers accountable, to disagree without being accused of belonging to the two dominant – but increasingly not viable – possibilities.

Simphiwe is not contained by this trap: being called reactionary or accused of reacting like a 'professional black' is not going to be enough to keep her quiet. As we all know if we pay attention, disagreeing and being offended by some of Zille's statements does not always mean that we are pawns in an ANC vs DA game. Members of the public can think for ourselves. Being critical of the decreasing alternatives offered by the ANC does not mean that we are DA sympathisers.

There is a world in between.

Part of what is both frightening and inspiring about Simphiwe is that she is really interested in examining what the world in between can contain, in building that Africa. There are many places, a 'range of templates'. It is simply not true that no real alternative is possible. Simphiwe's approach suggests that it will only exist once we create it, and there is more than one. Many of the existing alternatives are not real and do not get much public support and even less by way of votes because, although they pretend to be alternatives, they in fact are recognisable as something too similar to something else. So, for example, the United Democratic Movement, the Congress of the People (COPE), and the various breakaways from the Pan Africanist Congress are too similar to something we have seen and not voted for in droves, or too similar to that which we want to stop voting for, or may already have stopped voting for.

While there is a huge hunger for an alternative, or more suitably a series of alternatives, only new imaginative thinking can successfully 'fracture this metanarrative' of unitary nationalism post-1994, to use Barbara Boswell's formulation. This challenge that Simphiwe poses in her work, to imagine ourselves anew, to actively construct a new language and new terms of engagement holds the key to many of our hauntings. She is neither a politician nor does she have aspirations to public office. She does not need to do either in order to change the way we think. The best thinkers did not need to. Simphiwe is an example of the best kind of thinker. Perhaps if she wrote different kinds of genres we would recognise this, and call her a philosopher or a theorist. But because we pretend the terrain of the creative arts cannot do this work, we tell her to step back in place.

CHAPTER 7

Freeing the imagination

There is so much good music in the world, why has the world not changed for the better?

Simphiwe Dana

A good or great writer may refuse to accept any responsibility or morality that society wishes to impose on her. Yet the best and greatest of them know that if they abuse this hard-won freedom, it can only lead to bad art. There is an intricate web of morality, rigor, and responsibility that art, that writing itself, imposes on a writer.

Arundhati Roy

Children are born with wild imagination. You can see it when they play. Sometimes I feel like our education system is an exercise in disciplining the imagination.

AC Fick

The idea of a woman poised to fly, sometimes paying attention to her wings, is everywhere in Simphiwe Dana's music. Sometimes these wings are not in the best shape, but the woman always knows she will fly. In her first hit, which continues to be a firm favourite, 'Ndiredi', she declares that she is ready and strong enough to soar, and soar she does. But as we listen, it is very clear that she needs more than the right body and equipment to do so. Her language is very visual. We can almost see the dangers she narrowly escapes (the cliffs she almost falls off, the snake's tail she nearly steps on, the bearings she just about loses) as clearly as we hear her. These are all idioms, but she weaves them together poetically. When she speaks of almost losing herself, her choice is 'ukududa': aimless, hopeless wandering associated with physical and emotional distress. People afflicted in this manner are prayed for, slaughtered for and sedated. To this substantial list, she adds: 'I almost listened when s/he said I would not be able to'. They are of the same world. All of them can kill her.

The woman in 'Ndiredi' chooses to fly as an alternative to the abyss of self-loathing which would kill her if she stayed in this place. If you fall off a cliff, or get bitten by a snake, or wander aimlessly without sustenance or rest, you do die. Biko said 'You're either alive and proud, or you're dead. And if you're dead, you don't care anyway'. Flying away is part of how the persona in 'Ndiredi' chooses herself and her own. She does not run. She does not die. She decides that she is strong enough to fly. When she asks for umoya, both air and space, to fly, she leaves the narrative of her inferiority behind.

In this song, the landscape metaphors and Xhosa idioms do not exist at the level of the instrumental. They are not vehicles for telling the story. They are the story too, the architecture of the narrative, if you like. Nobody would say they only care about what the home they buy feels like. When we house-hunt, we know that the structure matters as much as what we bring into it. 'Ndiredi' requires the same shift in thinking about how the language is not just transportation but the very bones of the story. Later, in this chapter, I will say something about why this needs to be stated at all in relation to art at this juncture in South African history.

The same personality appears again in '*Zundiqondisise*', through the defiant self-ownership that asserts, with me paraphrasing rather than literally translating her: I never asked for your validation; you are neither my all, nor my responsibility. I do my things, my own way: enter, speak, exit, walk, pray, play and fly my way. Unlike '*Ndiredi*', '*Zundiqondisise*' is less about claiming space and flying off and more in the gesture of 'leave me alone to do my own thing'. In '*Ndim iqhawe* Part 2', again, we have a wounded hero(ine) with a broken wing who nonetheless will succeed in moving a mountain in order to fly again, if only in another life, the afterlife.

Wings, flight and freedom for Simphiwe, in different songs, echo similar and intersecting meanings. There is enough on the meanings of flight in her work to fill the kind of analysis that goes into a doctoral study. And she is working on her fourth album as I write this, so there is no guessing how many flying women will appear there. I have only mentioned a small selection of songs here to say something about her framework. Simphiwe subtly conceives of flying in her songs as part of imagining herself and her tribe anew. For her, the creative process of making music is not totally separated from imagining other possibilities of being a freer person in the world. These two acts of the imagination are closely related. I think of them as first cousins. They may even be siblings.

Flight in Simphiwe's music is about learning how to pattern the routes to self-love and freedom. This is part of why she returns to it again and again. And no matter what the song is about, flight always marks either grasping at joy or celebration. This is why Simphiwe's music makes people cry, because it takes the struggle to be a self-loving person seriously, as both personal and deeply political. At a time when consumer culture seduces us into a dangerous self-critical level that would have us change everything about ourselves, this is an astonishingly feminist choice. Yes, this is affirming. But it is much more than this. Listening to her, it is as though she has figured out how to move beyond braiding 'Beauty' and 'Pride' into each other, the two pillars of Black Consciousness in the creation of freedom, to actually fusing them into each other. In every song, it is hard to see where one ends and another starts. But if you understand the language well enough, this works for people living in the shadow of other violent hierarchies, such as homophobia, too. Most of us live in the places where different systems of power meet. In 1983, African American feminist law professor, Kimberlé Crenshaw gave the world the word 'intersectionality' to describe this meeting place of multiple power systems and identities.

A sustained analysis of 'flying' in Simphiwe Dana's work requires more than a chapter. It is not a motif or theme. It is a paradigm, the beginning of a language to speak about something urgent. Until she figures it out, and she may never realise whether she has, she will return to it again and again. This does not mean she has not created a paradigm, or 'theory', as we call it in the Humanities. It means she does not feel that she has finished creating it, even if what she has already given us is so rich.

Sometimes, artists' central concerns reoccur in their work not because the artists have heightened taste for this recurring motif (although it sometimes is this) and more because they are trying to do something quite important with it and have not finished the work. It is clear to me, for instance, that Nadine Gordimer's fascination with the white woman-black man romance/activist combination in very different novels over several decades is not just about revisiting a relationship she may or may not have had with an activist, writer, Black man and mining it for metaphor. It is not just autobiographical impetus as some scholars of her work suggest, but a niggling working out in words of something very specific about the meeting places of race and sexuality. When Rustum Kozain writes so many 'stones' into his poems, he is not really thinking about apartheid township missiles. When I mentioned it, he admitted that he had never noticed all the stones in his poems.

In the conversations I have had with Simphiwe over the last few years, I don't remember her talking about flying except when we were discussing the kind that involves airports. It is not as if she has specific aviation interests or slips in flying metaphors when we speak about food, sex, politics or parenting. There would be nothing wrong with this if she did.

When French literary scholar Ronald Barthes wrote of the author of any and all texts as dead, he meant to draw attention to how creative texts are influenced by many contexts and bring to life entire universes that weren't directly planned by musicians. The artist and her life does not become the authority on her work. Therefore, flying is everywhere in Simphiwe's music, but she doesn't spend all her time thinking about flying. The music is its own universe. Perhaps what flying stands for in her music, she expresses differently in her day-to-day life. I certainly think so, as the soft feminist chapter shows.

How we think about the arts and aesthetic universes in contemporary South Africa disregards the very wealth that works of the imagination offer. I often hear readers ask essayists to 'say it in simple language, in a sentence or two'. Often, the essayist responds along the lines of 'if I could do that, I would not have written five books on it'. This is not just a case of creatives with verbal diarrhoea. When philosophy PhD and founder of an African feminist press, Bibi Bakare-Yusuf speaks about the anti-intellectual wave sweeping across Nigeria, I often feel she should say 'across South Africa' instead. In our public culture, there is a highly audible disdain for anything that requires thinking, with the accusation of 'over-thinking' and 'over-analysing' thrown out to anybody who will not 'simplify' what they do or toe the line. It is resistance against thinking-feeling. It does not matter, for my purposes here, that I have many ideas about where this comes from, historically. This resistance is linked to what Simphiwe Dana speaks about when she notes that South Africa does not like or get her. It is because her work invites the very thing we have built an identity around resisting in the last decade. When we are most resistant to thinking, we cannot be responsive to transformative art. We pretend that is because of what we associate with the Thabo Mbeki presidency, which we sometimes call intellectual arrogance. When we say so we forget that we called him 'our president-in-waiting' when Mandela was at the helm, and that we then voted him into the presidency twice. This resistance to turning inward also lies behind two other contradictions in contemporary South Africa: one on Biko and the other on misogyny.

I am astounded by how we all claim to read Biko while skin lighteners have returned with a vengeance in expensive 'fade' creams, and adverts on public broadcasters sell the erasure of the dark, nappy and oily. We believe in and circulate colonialist racist images about the rest of the continent and, therefore, always indirectly about ourselves. All the while, we allow people to simultaneously act like middle-class gangsters in public spaces while claiming Black Consciousness allegiance. As though Biko and his comrades did not leave enough of a written legacy for us to be able to see how political our treatment of ourselves and others *always* is.

We also constantly boast about the high mobility of middle-class women in South Africa, the high numbers represented compared to most other places in the world, and our proto-feminist Constitution. At the same time, we don't think we are ready for a woman in the Union Buildings. Similarly, the accusation of rape, and his reckless responses to it, are not serious enough to keep a powerful man out of our highest office. We reward public misogyny but call for men to march against rape, failing to understand why the rape statistics refuse to decline.

What would it mean for South Africans to take the project of turning inward seriously, feeding imagination and doing the collective self-reflexive work that great art often invites? What would it mean in relation to the great self-hating and misogynist decisions we publicly endorse, or at least desist from questioning?

Against this backdrop, I disagree with Simphiwe about South Africa not loving, appreciating or getting her. Her musical project, her aesthetic choices, the layers of meaning in her work require that we do the two things that are least fashionable in South Africa right now: that we invest in the intellectual-emotional work that comes with taking ourselves seriously and as part of that process take our cultural production seriously. Societies with healthy collective consciousness take their creative production, their culture, seriously. We are not that society. If we collectively turned inward, held our leaders really accountable, and took responsibility for our complicity with violence, we might implode. We might also finally have a chance at addressing the various forms of institutional violence we live amidst whether they be class, race, gender or sexuality-based. Most of them are intersectional.

Let me turn, for a while, to how we *do* treat our cultural production in South Africa today. By cultural production, I mean works of the imagination.

How many times have you tuned into your regular morning, afternoon or evening radio show as you drove about and listened to a caller bemoan the state of a popular music genre, usually kwaito, for being repetitive or empty of substance? Perhaps you nodded in agreement and even chuckled along, tickled by the caller's hyperbolic expression and charmed by his wit. Maybe you were the caller.

This scenario has played itself out in my life so many times I have long lost count. Sometimes I chuckle at the turn of phrase even as I change the channel or press play so a kwaito song can play instead. I find the constant repetition of this claim quite interesting, especially considering who and where we are in South Africa today. I like kwaito as a genre and am quite attached to it. I am not a fan of much of the latest productions, but my distaste is seldom provoked by the same things as the irate, somewhat dramatic caller.

Many South Africans seem to believe that art forms should have substance, that creative products do not justify their existence by their mere presence in the world. I have lost count of the number of times people claim that they like someone's music or writing or painting because it had a 'message' or a 'story'. This is why local authors sell so well that we now have an abundance of full-time writers with paid up bonds and medical aid, who never have to worry about their children's fees. South Africans love their stories and they show it. Feel free to substitute 'actors/musicians' and 'theatre tickets/CDs' where I have written 'authors' and 'books' for the same effect. I am wishing out aloud. The truth is that most artists have 'day jobs' or 'side gigs' to survive.

This preoccupation with art, with meaning, relevance and substance makes sense given varied episodes in our pasts. We are all aware of how political art was used as part of the liberation project against slavery, colonialism and apartheid. Although South African Black art under apartheid is often paraded under labels like 'committed art' and 'protest art', to underscore that it was not 'art for art's sake' but art crafted and used in the service of liberation, attention to the pathways of global art show that, in fact, South Africa is not unique in this position. There are many meeting places for art and politics.

Many with a historical eye on culture also remind us of the many ways in which pre-colonial and surviving African senses of the aesthetic were very often linked to the social, the political, the spiritual and the erotic. In other words, very seldom has art been for its own sake, although previous generations seem to have been less queasy about enjoying the works of the imagination produced in their time. Oral literature scholars remind us of the way in which previous oral forms were open to various functionalities. In his writings on African humanism as well as in his autobiography, *Down Second Avenue*, Ezekiel Mphahlele (later Es'kia Mphahlele) points to the role of storytelling as socialisation into political, economic, familial and spiritual realms. In other words, while the stories were told in elaborate stylistics, and could be frightening or hilarious, depending on the skills of the teller, the audience were engaged in various human theatres at the same time as they listened and interacted. I am using the past tense, but this is true of more than one epoch. Even though societies which historically valued the oral over the written were deemed inferior by those who colonised them, in different parts of the world, we now know several things about stories are similar, whether these are written down or transmitted orally. One of the things we know is that stories are not just the sum total of what happens. Meaning also lies in how we are told the stories. Historians know this well. As Hayden White reminds us in his seminal study *Metahistory*, there are always different ways of making sense of the same story, and each telling also braids interpretation into the narrative. People who like words like 'facts' and 'objectivity' are highly irritated by this kind of argument: that the arrangement of the facts is subjective.

Consider the following paraphrased story, which made me chuckle when I first read it. It is a Native American story, captured in Canadian historian, Ronald Wright's *Stolen Continents*. A long time ago, when the Creator Spirit decided to people the earth, He-She-It gave different heightened talents and sensibilities to humans from different places in the world. To those with exceptional capacity for memory and abstraction, He-She-It gave oral tales. Having endowed other humans with weaker memories and fascination with precision, the Creator Spirit gave these people books since they could not be expected (trusted) with the intricacies of oral narrative.

When you read this story, you almost feel sorry for those cultures that have longstanding written traditions, a visible permanent marker of what they lack in imagination. But you have heard this story before. You may have heard it this way: While God started making the first few people at about the same time, they did not develop and civilise themselves at the same pace. Those who were at the cutting edge of civilisation developed reliable forms of keeping record: writing, which eventually took the form of books. The less developed were stuck in oral narratives, which are unreliable because each person changes the story in the telling. This rendition turns your original sympathies upside down.

People who like facts get this: some societies have written traditions; others have oral narratives. But we know that this listing of facts misses much about the two stories above, what they share as well as the ways in which they differ. It removes the feelings each story elicited. The first two stories centre the teller's world as the reference points from which to read the world. They may be very different because of what we now know about the historical formation of the world. But each teller comes from a society that starts with him/her.

The stories we tell about ourselves matter. So, as South Africans in 2012, we may want artistic expression with a message and a story, but very often we turn away and avert our gaze from this very content we claim to value. This is because South Africa has several simultaneous relationships with works of the imagination. There is the impulse I have outlined above, which makes us demand that art has purpose.

At the same time, we create a false opposition between the value of works of the imagination, on the one hand, and scientific and economic activity, on the other. Societies that take themselves seriously, who are at the centre of their own universes, realise that this is an unnecessary dichotomy. There is no opposition. We were such societies once.

The dominant paradigm on art in contemporary South Africa is of art as something flighty and superficial. In the main, art is entertainment, where entertainment offers escape and not reflection or transformation. In many instances, art is both treated in this manner and lambasted when it is perceived to successfully function only as escape. If that seems like a contradiction, it is because that is the point. Consider the following examples.

Scenario A is at a GALA dinner or Awards Ceremony with a fusion cuisine, five course meal, served with bottled water and fine South African wine. At your elegant table the striking menu and programme bear a resemblance to the invitation to which you had to RSVP, as well as to tonight's decor. The racially diverse audience is expensively perfumed, turned out in 'formal or traditional' outfits and in high spirits. Somebody worth celebrating is being honoured. There is an MC or a Programme Director, depending on who is paying for the event. The conversation flows freely in between announcements. If protocol is to be observed, waiting time will be part of the event. This does not necessarily mean that the proceedings will start late, however. It may just mean that you have to arrive early at 18h30 for a 19h00 event, as per invitation. While you wait, and in between the 'important' parts of the programme such as speeches and award acceptance, a band plays a set or two. Sometimes a poet or group performs. If

140

this is not a music or literature event, you ignore the artists who play background music to your dinner. Every now and again, a few people at other tables clap in appreciation. Mostly, you eat, chat, play with your phone, read the menu and wait for the MC/ Programme Director to reappear.

Scenario B involves a visual artist who is minding her business, making her art, who is then approached for permission for her work to be used on the cover of a book that is neither about her nor her work. The artist names the price, is paid and the artwork appears on the cover of a book of essays. Much deliberation went into choosing the artwork and artists as well as approaching her for the cover art. However, beyond the copyright credit, there is no mention of the artwork. It is now mere decoration. Academics in the Social Sciences are notorious for this, so are essayists generally.

Scenario C refers to a photographer who opens a publication to discover the unaccredited use of his work all over an article that may or may not be directly about the subject of his photograph. If he contacts the publication, which is usually a profitable outfit within an established stable, he is told his images were simply pulled from the internet and 'everybody does it'. Sometimes the piece of work is not a photograph, but some other genre like a substantial extract from an essay. Many South African artists have first-hand experience of this.

Scenario D involves a professional couple interested in acquiring specific visual works of art. They have an investment portfolio and drive luxury cars. When they are introduced to the artist whose work they were admiring, at less than 10 per cent of their car price tags, they try to bargain on the price of the painting. The artwork will significantly increase in value. Their cars will decline considerably.

Scenario E is an offer that can be summed up in a sentence: Please come and work for us for free and as payment we will give you exposure.

All five scenarios are regular experiences for working artists of various kinds in South Africa, and they are all underpinned by the same assumptions. The first is that artistic production is not work.

141

The second is that making art is not a real career or job. Third, art is for fun and escape. Therefore, when people pay attention to art, they are 'supporting' the artist, or The Arts. They never talk of 'supporting' their lawyer, doctor or therapist but they pay the amount required by these professionals without bargaining.

The people who see nothing wrong with any of this behaviour may be the same drivers agreeing with the radio caller who chastised kwaito for being without message. Yet, in their interaction with various forms of art listed in my five scenarios, they have deliberately chosen not to interact with art as though it matters. They have acted as though payment is the only validation, pretended the message does not matter, or averted their gaze from the 'story'. The point is not that we should feel guilty about 'being uncultured', nor that we are a country of hypocrites. And if you bought this book, you are probably someone who pays to see and/or hear Simphiwe Dana, and you are obviously someone who thinks books are worth spending money on. So, you may well argue that I am preaching to the choir. And you would be right, to a certain extent. Yet, I am also pretty sure that you recognised the truth in one or more of the scenarios above, even if you are not an actor in any of them.

What would happen if we *collectively* thought about the creative differently, beyond the realm of our personal favourites, if we responded with repulsion at the suggestion that the Ministry of Arts and Culture is a throwaway space, not a key political appointment? Perhaps we could allow ourselves to be challenged even in ways that we would rather not be.

Simphiwe Dana's music achieves brilliantly what works of the imagination very often do: she activates a range of ways of being in the world. She invites us to question while we dance, choose differently while she moves us to tears. Simphiwe's work re-ignites or inspires, depending on who we are, a desire for more freedom, to be so much more than what is available. But the real magic is that she encourages this and sometimes provokes us into this impulse, without degrading where we are now.

For Simphiwe Dana, as for many people, creative production

provides many opportunities for growth and exploration. Works of the imagination are sites of quest and discovery. They bring the possibility of change to both the musician, Simphiwe, as well as for those of us who listen and are affected by her music. The creative arts are also a very important site for the staging of critical ideas and a critical consciousness. Few people know this as well as South Africans, precisely because we have previously saturated our collective consciousness with this very discussion. At the same time, we know and avoid some of the real challenges that great art presents. It is not that we really believe, collectively, that joy cannot also be transformative or that we think pleasure is expendable. Anybody who is familiar with the elaborate artistry present in contemporary Black dance styles, the dizzying speed at which they change, and the complicated language of response that they structure and restructure, cannot at the same time think South Africans don't get that pleasure is complicated.

Although AC Fick was speaking about literature specifically when he made the comments I summarise below, what he said can be applied to other engagements with creative genres, not just in literary expression. His comments unintentionally speak very directly to South African relationships with music and Simphiwe Dana.

AC Fick reminds us of the importance of thinking about literacy and knowledge as more than just functional. Casting his mind back to our arrival at university for the first time in February 1990, regardless of what kind of education we had prior to this as Black students, he notes our deliberate and direct investment in the project of thinking for ourselves. Part of this required a sense of ourselves that was very different from what was conceivable in the University of Cape Town we entered, in his and my case. Yes, this was partly because this was late apartheid, and also a few days after Nelson and Winnie Mandela walked hand in hand in public for the first time in nearly three decades. But it was also because thinking was important in and of itself for us. Today, public and official education discourse stresses the functionality of knowledge. Here, knowledge and concrete skills need to be shown to have a specific future application: train them so that they can neatly slot into the job market. This approach, Fick notes, does not allow for nurturing an imagination, dreaming and learning to understand the world as valuable and necessary skills for active citizenship. Reading and intellectual discussion are dismissed as snobbery, arrogance and not seen as engaging complexly with ideas. Part of what we undervalue in this process is critical thinking, forgetting that empathy is an effect of critical thinking. Instead, we proceed with the assumption that vocabulary is the same thing as understanding. If we take this connection between critical thinking and empathy, perhaps it makes sense that the Marikana horror could happen in 2012 South Africa.

Works of the imagination still offer the possibility of re-learning how to collectively embrace critical thinking and thinking for ourselves. Fick reminds us that critical thinking collectives are harder to govern totally. Part of what makes Simphiwe Dana so compelling for me, part of why I had to write this book, is that she is almost impossible to govern. While she does not identify as an anarchist as I write this, she is her own person. She will not play by many of the rules that our society churns out. She thinks and speaks for herself, recognises her wounds, but is nobody's victim. She cannot be silenced and she will not be made to speak about herself. Often struggling with things in public that others think are better left to the private, Simphiwe lives her truth and takes chances. Many of these choices are difficult. But she is nobody's puppet.

Simphiwe's consistent commitment in her music is the question: how do I use this experience to think and see the world differently? Her music is not straightforward. It perfectly fits in the mode of what Fick calls creative products 'that are volatile in their relationship with the world in order to engage the world': they offer challenges to our senses of self where 'each encounter is a different confrontation', offering a different possibility of discovery and subversion. This is akin to what Barbara Boswell calls 'creative re-visioning' when she writes about Black South African women artists in another genre. Boswell defines this creative inclination as 'the ability to re-envision or re-imagine what is possible to achieve in [our] lifetime'.

CHAPTER 8

Beautiful complexities – Departures

Often, the most important part of our human existence is our ability to imagine.

Bibi Bakare-Yusuf

Speaking to Penny Lebyane about Simphiwe Dana, the photographer and writer, Victor Dlamini spoke about the musician's 'beautiful complexity'. He commented that although people had not bought copies of *One Love Movement on Bantu Biko Street*, that CD would become a reference point, and a classic that people would return to again, and again. He spoke about it as a layered album and of *Kulture Noir* as an album that is a canvass where you get the colours of the music. While I agree with Dlamini about both albums, I am also aware of how out of step with Victor's evaluation the public response was. I also know how hard it must have been to produce something that transcendental and be met with both hostility and near silence.

I remember how wounded she felt the December immediately after its release. She was also startled by the very personal attack that cultural critic and essayist, Bongani Madondo published in place of the review his readers expected. In the article, the usually perceptive Madondo launched into a bizarre personal diatribe in which he commented disapprovingly on Simphiwe's personal and love life with her former partner with whom she had children. There was no evidence in that piece that Madondo had even listened to the CD. I suspect that he had, in fact, listened to it, but had simply chosen not to engage it at all. This is a writer's prerogative. However, it would have been more honest for a writer of Madondo's calibre to be open about this choice.

I was taken aback by this response from Madondo in 'Dear Soul Sistah', even though the bulk of the responses to Simphiwe's second album *did* make sense. Let me clarify. I was not surprised by the specific article because it is not uncommon to have women artists' lives commented on, rather than their work, whether this is done with approval or derision. The visual artist and feminist curator, Nontobeko Ntombela argues that this is a very effective way of deflecting from the content of transgressive women's work. Therefore, often, rather than write a review or engage the ideas and techniques of a woman whose artwork unsettles us, reviewers write pieces about *her*. In *The One Love Movement on Bantu Biko Street*, Simphiwe was dealing with thoughts, ways of being, possibilities and offering an invitation to imagine ourselves in ways that people were not ready to hear. It was time. But often we flinch and turn away from precisely what we most urgently need to hear. What was surprising and disturbing was the fact that Madondo, a writer who has consistently stared straight at the difficult and discomfiting in artistic expression from the African world before, was its author. He was to choose differently this time, a fact which still holds some measure of mystery for me, all these years later.

Perhaps the reason Ms Dana's third album is so awe-inspiring is because she wrote it to affirm herself, as she has suggested in interviews. Maybe the same way that people may have picked up on the sadness she felt when she wrote the second album, we pick up on the affirmation when we listen to the third one. Rather than break down, she worked and gave herself what she needed to begin to heal. Both *Kulture Noir* and love came at the tail end of that healing. The range of feelings that saturate every note and every lyric on her third album are connected to this. Simphiwe is an artist, able to turn anything into magic. It is her alchemy.

The One Love Movement on Bantu Biko Street as an album, but also the song for which it is named, is a beautiful assertion of presence, as much as it is a declaration of a generation that they need to be here and proud. In the song, the singer's purse may be empty but it is a beautiful purse that she will carry as she walks down that glorious imaginary Bantu Biko Street. She will feel good and proud as she reminds us that Biko '*wathi qala ngaphakathi*'. The song, like many others in her repertoire, assumes that you will bring a range of intertextual references to make sense of her. But your enjoyment and feeling are not dependent on the intellectual recognition of the references. The woman singing about carrying her purse knows what it means to carry your purse, *uzimisele*, walking down the street, but she is also foregrounding Black Consciousness's insistence that interiority matters. In her music, in true spirit of self-love and generosity of spirit that is so evident in early Black Consciousness art, but so denied in much that goes by that appellation now, Simphiwe knows that transformation requires power and love, that imagining herself and us anew is critical to survival.

I have wanted to write this book for a long time. I am glad that I have done so, and this time, I really understand what writers sometimes mean when they say they needed to write it and are able to release it with little anxiety. It is very different from the book I imagined it would be. Having wanted to write it, when the opportunity was generously presented to me, I was thrilled. I was at the tail end of an upheaval in my life. Little did I know that what I mistook for a climbing was in fact a precipice. Every writing project has its gifts.

When I asked the novelist Thando Mgqolozana, who loves the

track '*Mayine*' as passionately as I am obsessed with '*Ilolo*', why he liked the song so much, he BBM'd back:

> It has to do with the space in which I was finding myself, as a person as well as a writer. When I discovered the song, I was writing in a way I never thought I could. I was immensely relieved by this. As a person, I had been fighting to stay sane for years, when I discovered this song I felt a kind of mental strength I had not had in a long, long time. I felt like *Mayine* was the language I needed to articulate my recently gained confidence and health. I was also aware that the writer and singer of this song had gone through her own struggles. I felt that with this song, in particular, she had found a coded language with which to tell us, and herself, that the time had come – a corner had been turned. In the African community, there are rainmakers/callers. They go up the mountain to 'pray' for this. But it is only when it is starting to pour down that a cry *Mayineeeeee* can be heard. I love the song for this depth, this sensitiveness. The closest thing to it is Stimela or 'End of the Road' (Medley).

Perhaps '*Mayine*' is a language to articulate all our transitions to a freer life.

Zukiswa Wanner noted that although she had been blown away with the recognition that 'an artist was born' when she first listened to Simphiwe's debut album, seeing her in recent performances and listening to the two offerings that followed *Zandisile*, Wanner changed her mind. In 2011, Wanner writes:

> As I conclude this piece while listening to Dana's *Ndimi Nawe* I realize that if indeed I was right about a star being born when I listened to Dana's *Zandisile*, that may not necessarily be true now. Because through her music and her connection with her audience whether via CD or at a live performance, Dana is not a star. She is a planet all on her own.

Like Wanner, I am drawn to write about Simphiwe at length not simply because I am a fan, a neighbour, or a woman who lives in the same country and at the same historical moment as Ms Dana. Instead, I have written this book because I think she is an integral figure of our times, whose ideas in her collective genres require more sustained interrogation and engagement with. I did not want her genius to be relegated to the footnotes of history because although she is everywhere today, I know how quickly genius can disappear from public view. What if she decided to become a reclusive monk and no longer produce public work?

As someone who has self-identified as a feminist since high school, I am also drawn to a certain kind of renegade behaviour. Even when the contradictions, transgressions and actions do not make complete sense to me, I am drawn to women who own themselves, as well as women who take the risks in order to be able to do that. I know that renegade behaviour is policed, commented on, belittled, and deliberately misunderstood. One of the gifts feminism and academic literary training have bestowed upon me is that they long freed me from the desire for approval. I neither need to approve of every aspect of a person's life to appreciate their value, nor want to. Patricia McFadden writes:

> I craft my own identity as an everyday experience; I have given myself licence to do just that – to re-shape those aspects that made me up which I have grown to like and enjoy; usually the bonds I share with my siblings and familiars; and to vigorously shed the stuff that my mother, aunts and a multitude of women in my community insisted would turn me into a 'decent woman' – knock-kneed but decent nonetheless. In the process I have shrugged my beautiful feminist shoulders and strode over that sloughed, oppressive skin – emerging after half a century in my brilliant, gorgeous feminist garb – free and flying as high as I can get.

I may be a decade away from half a century of life as I finish writing this, but these words resonate with me.

I think we throw away women who push boundaries in our society, even though we reward men who do so, often to our peril. Even in the frenzy of academic and other essays on prominent figures in South Africa, I have noticed how few of these are of women – including the ones that we claim to adore without contradiction. While bemoaning the paucity of books about women in public who matter is valid, when we can do something about it, as writers, and choose not to, we are playing victim.

I have written *A Renegade Called Simphiwe* because writing is how we think about and through a whole range of realities. Writing is one of the ways we say things matter.

It would be a shame to forget to see her music next to her poems, newspaper opinion editorials, social media contributions, graphic design and Information Technology influences. A biography would provide more details on her private life, try to flatten what she says and does so that it can all 'make sense' in a neat chronological way. Biographies are hugely important and necessary. But they are not the only way to make sense.

I have found a different creative non-fictional genre better suited to my ends, although I look forward to reading biographies about her. It has been a really rewarding experience to engage creatively and intellectually with Simphiwe's public worlds. It has also challenged many things about how I usually write. In the final analysis, a creative-intellectual portrait in words seems like an apt engagement with the many faces of Simphiwe as well as with the enormous gift of her own creative intellect.

Bibliography

Akomfrah, J (1996) *The Last Angel of History*, Icarus Film
Distributors, London
AIT Nigeria (2010) 'Bibi Bakare-Yusuf', *Focus Nigeria*, 18
December broadcast
Baderoon, G (2005) *The Dream in the Next Body*, Kwela,
Roggebaai
Baderoon, G (2005) *The Museum of Ordinary Life*, Tranan,
Stockholm
Baderoon, G (2006) *A Hundred Silences, Kwela*, Roggebaai
Baderoon, G (2010) 'On looking and not looking', *Mail &
Guardian*, 9 March
Bakare-Yusuf, B (accessed 30 March 2012) 'Of mini-skirts and
morals: Social control in Nigeria', *Our Africa: Through
women's eyes*. 22 February http://www.opendemocracy.
net/5050/bibi-bakare-yusuf/of-mini-skirts-and-morals-social-
control-in-nigeria
Barthes, R (1977) *Image-Music-Text*, Farrar, Straus and Giroux,
New York
Berger, J (1972) *Ways of Seeing*, Penguin, London
Biko, Steve (1978) *I Write What I Like*, Borweadean, London
Bongo Maffin (1996) *Leaders of D'Gong*, EMI
Bongo Maffin (1997) *Final Entry*, EMI
Bongo Maffin (1998) *The Concerto*, SONY BMG

Bongo Maffin (2001) *Bongolution*, Gallo

Bongo Maffin (2005) *New Construction*. Gallo

Boswell, B (2010) 'Black South African women writers: Narrating the self, narrating the nation', Unpublished PhD dissertation, University of Maryland, College Park

Braudy, L (1986) *The Frenzy of Renown*, Oxford University Press, Oxford

Crenshaw, Kimberlé (1991) 'Mapping the margins: Intersectionality, identity politics and violence against women of color', *Stanford Law Review*, 43, pp. 1241–1279

Dana, Simphiwe (2004) *Zandisile*, Gallo

Dana, Simphiwe (2006) *The One Love Movement on Bantu Biko Street*, Gallo

Dana, Simphiwe (2010) *Kulture Noir*, Gallo

Dana, Simphiwe (2011) *Live at the Lyric*, Live DVD

Dana, Simphiwe (2012) 'State of Emergency'

David McKnight, M (2007) 'Afro-futurism and Post-Soul Possibility in Black Popular Music', *African American Review*, 41 (4), pp. 695–707

Dworkin, A (1987) *Intercourse*, Basic Books, New York

Dyer, R (1979) *Stars*, British Film Institute, London

Evans, J and Hesmondhalgh, D (2005) *Understanding Media: Inside celebrity*, McGraw-Hill Education, Columbus, OH

Fanon, F (trans. Richard Philcox) (2007) [1952] *Black Skin, White Mask*, Grove Press, New York

Fick, AC (2012) 'Correlations between logic and language: a material history of literacy', Unpublished paper presented at the *Teaching them to read: argument, explanation and logic in undergraduate teaching in South Africa Colloquium*, 1–7 August, University of the Witwatersrand, Johannesburg.

Forum for the Empowerment of Women (FEW) (accessed 15 September 2010) 'FEW is angered by Minister's reaction', available at http://www.few.org.za/index.php?option=com_content&view=article&id=107:few-is-angered-by-the-ministers-reaction&catid=19:press-release&Itemid=29

Gender DynamiX (Accessed 15 September 2010) 'Gender
DynamiX speaks out against Xingwana's bigotry', available
at http://www.few.org.za/index.php?option=com_content&vi
ew=article&catid=19:press-release&id=105:gender-dynamix-
speaks-out-against-xingwanas-bigotry&Itemid=29&layout=de
fault&date=2010-10-01

Gqola, P D (2006) 'Re/imagining ways of seeing: Making and
speaking selves through Zanele Muholi's eyes', in *Only Half a
Picture*, STE, Johannesburg

Gqola, P D (2011) 'Unconquered and insubordinate: Embracing
Black feminist intellectual activist legacies', in *Becoming
Worthy Ancestors: Archive, public deliberation and identity in
South Africa*, ed Xolela Mangcu, pp. 67–88, Wits University
Press Johannesburg

Gqola, P D and Baderoon, G (2010) 'Spotlight Interview: Gabeba
Baderoon speaks to Pumla Dineo Gqola about the joys,
inspirations and textures of writing and being read', *SABLE
LitMag* 14, pp. 17–33

Habermas, J (1989) [1962] *The Structural Transformation of the
Public Sphere: An inquiry into a category of bourgeois society*,
MIT Press, Cambridge, MA

Hall, S (1996) *Questions of Culture and Identity*, Sage,
Thousand Oaks

Hall, S (1997) *Representation: cultural representations and
signifying practices*, Sage, Thousand Oaks

Handlarski, D (2011) 'Re-sisters: South African Women's
Literature'. Unpublished PhD Dissertation, York University,
Toronto, Ontario

Holborn, LE, G (2011) *First Steps to Healing the South African
Family*. South African Institute of Race Relations Report,
Johannesburg

Joint Working Group (accessed 19 September 2010) 'Open Letter
to Minister Lulu Xingwana from activists and civil society
groupings', Available at http://2009.oia.co.za/glbt/open-letter-
to-minister-lulu-xingwana-from-activists-and-civil-society-
groupings/

Khumalo, A and Wanner, Z (2010) *8115: A Prisoner's Home*, Penguin, Johannesburg

Lorde, A (1982) *Zami: A new spelling of my name*, The Crossing Press, New York

Lorde, A (1984) *Sister Outsider: Essays and speeches*, Ten Speed Press, Berkeley, CA

Mapule, T (2009) 'Celebrity, commodification and photography: A textual analysis of *Heat* magazine', Unpublished research paper, Media Studies Department, University of the Witwatersrand.

Mashile, L (2005) *In a Ribbon of Rhythm*, Oshun, Cape Town & Mutloatse Arts Trust, Observatory

Mashile, L (2008) *Flying above the Sky*, Lebogang Mashile, Johannesburg

Masina, N L (2010) 'Black like me: Representations of Black women placed in contemporary South African magazines', Unpublished MA thesis, Media Studies, University of the Witwatersrand

Mazibuko, L (2012) 'How the DA is using e-tools to remake South African politics', excerpt from a speech delivered at the Freudrich Naumann Foundation Workshop, Global Media Forum 2012, Bonn, Germany

Mazwai, Thandiswa (2004) *Zabalaza*, CD, Gallo

Mazwai, Thandiswa (2009) *Ibokwe*, CD, Gallo

Mazwai, Thandiswa (2010) *Dance of the Forgotten Tree*, Live DVD, Gallo

McFadden, P (2011) 'Resisting the neo-colonial/neo-liberal collusion: Reclaiming our lives, our futures', Unpublished public lecture presented at the African Gender Institute, University of Cape Town, October

Molebatsi, N and d'Abdon, R (2007) 'From poetry to floetry: Music's influence in the spoken word art of young South Africa', *Muziki: Journal of Music Research in Africa*, 4 (2), pp. 171–177

Mphahlele, E (1959) *Down Second Avenue*, Faber & Faber, London

Peterson, B and Suleman, R (2009) *Zulu Love Letter: A screenplay*, Wits University Press, Johannesburg

Peterson, B (2012) 'Dignity, memory and the future under siege: Reconciliation and nation-building in post-apartheid South Africa', in *The New Violent Cartography: Geo-analysis after the aesthetic turn*, eds Opondo, SO and Shapiro, MJ, pp. 229–248, Routledge, London

Redmond, Sand Holmes, S (2008) *Stardom and Celebrity: A reader*, Sage, Thousand Oaks, CA

Rojek, C (2001) *Celebrity*, Reaktion Books, London

Roy, A (1997) *The God of Small Things*, Harper Collins, New York

Roy, A (2007) *The Cost of Living*, Random House, New York

Roy, A (2002) *Power Politics*, South End Press, Cambridge, MA.

Salo, E (2003) 'Negotiating gender and personhood in the new South Africa', *European Journal of Cultural Studies*, 6 (3), pp. 345–365

Shoncyin, L (2010) *The Secret Lives of Baba Segi's Wives*, Cassava Republic Press, Abuja

Spencer, L (2009) 'Young, black and female in post-apartheid South Africa', *Scrutiny2* 14 (1), pp. 66–78

Tamale, S (2003) 'Out of the Closet: Unveiling Sexuality Discourses in Uganda', *Feminist Africa* 2 http://agi.ac.za/sites/agi.ac.za/files/fa_2_standpoint_3.pdf

Tourè (accessed 10 October 2012) 'Lauryn Hill Interview with Fuse TV at Rock the Bells 2010, NYC', http://www.waterblocknyc.com/2010/09/video-lauryn-hill-interview-with-fuse.html

Turner, G (2004) *Understanding Celebrity*, Sage, London

Tyrangiel, J (accessed 10 October 2012) 'Andy was right', *Time*, 25 December http://www.time.com/time/magazine/article/0,9171,1570780,00.html

Walker, A (1986) *Revolutionary Petunias and Other Poems*, Harcourt Brace Janovich, New York

Wanner, Z (accessed 10 March 2011) 'African Writer's Corner: A conversation with Zukiswa Wanner', *Pambazuka News*

427: *African Unity: Feeling with Nkrumah, thinking with Nyerere*, 9 April 2009 http://www.pambazuka.org/en/category/African_Writers/55469

Wanner, Z (2006) *The Madams*, Oshun, Cape Town

Wanner, Z (2008) *Behind Every Successful Man*, Kwela, Roggebaai

Wanner, Z (2010) *Men of the South*, Kwela, Roggebaai

Wanner, Z (accessed 12 October 2012) 'South Africa', *Guernica: A magazine of art and politics*. 17 January http://www.guernicamag.com/daily/zukiswa_wanner_south_africa/

Wanner, Z (accessed 10 June 2012) 'Simphiwe: South Africa's emerging force', *Africa Review*. 1 April 2011

Wa Thiong'o, N (2012) 'Speaking my language', Address to the 2012 *Sunday Times* Literary Awards, 21 June

Weber, M (2007) 'The nature of charismatic domination', in *Stardom and Celebrity: A reader,* eds S Holmes and S Redmond, pp. 17–14, Sage, London

Wete, B (accessed 15 July 2012) 'Norah Jones: The women are complex too interview', *Complex*. June/July http://www.complex.com/music/2012/06/norah-jones-women-are-complex-too-interview

White, H (1975) *Metahistory: The historical imagination in nineteenth-century Europe,* Johns Hopkins University Press, Baltimore, Maryland

Williams, P (1991) *The Alchemy of Race and Rights: The diary of a law professor,* Harvard University Press, Cambridge, MA

Williams, R (1977) *Marxism and Literature*, Oxford University Press, Oxford

Wonci, SV (2011) 'A conversation with Ingrid Masondo', *Agenda* 25, pp. 50–58

Wright, R (1992) *Stolen Continent: The 'new world' through Indian eyes since 1492*, Houghton Mifflin, New York

Wright, R (2005) *Stolen Continents: Five hundred years of conquest and resistance in the Americas* First Mariner Books, New York

Yates, K A and Gqola PD (1998) 'Some kind of madness: Mamphela Ramphele on being Black and transgressive', *Agenda* 37, pp. 90–95

Zille, H (accessed 25 October 2012) 'There are no short-cuts to social cohesion', an excerpt from a speech to the National Social Cohesion Summit in Kliptown, 4 July http://www.da.org.za/newsroom.htm?action=view-news-item&id=10919

Zille, H (accessed 25 October 2012), 'Personal reflections on three weeks of "outrage"', http://www.da.org.za/newsroom.htm?action=view-news-item&id=10542

Zille, H (2012) 'Twitter storm is clouding the real issue', *Politicsweb*, 28 March

Zimmerman, P (1995) *Reel Families: A Social History of Amateur Film*, Indiana University Press, Bloomington

Author biography

Pumla Dineo Gqola is the author of *What is Slavery to Me? Postcolonial/Slave memory in Post-apartheid South Africa* (published by Wits Press in 2010) and editor of *Regarding Winnie: Feminism, race and nation in global representations of Winnie Madikizela Mandela* (forthcoming with Cassava Republic Press). She has written non-fiction and opinion pieces for *Pambazuka, Mail & Guardian, The Weekender* and *City Press* as well as the British publications *BBC Focus on Africa, SABLE* and *Drum* (UK) and short stories in literary journals and books published in South Africa, USA and UK. Pumla holds MA degrees from the universities of Cape Town and Warwick, UK and a PhD from the Ludwig Maximillian University of Munich, Germany. She is associate professor of African literary and gender studies at the University of the Witwatersrand.